JUNIOR COLLEGE DISTRICT
of St. Louis-St. Louis County
LIBRARY
7508 Forsyth Blvd.
St. Louis, Missouri 63105

THE GREAT AWAKENING IN THE
MIDDLE COLONIES

THE GREAT AWAKENING
IN THE MIDDLE
COLONIES

By

CHARLES HARTSHORN MAXSON

Assistant Professor of Political Science in the
University of Pennsylvania

Gloucester, Mass.

PETER SMITH

1958

PREFACE

Centennial celebrations of what Jonathan Edwards called the "Revival of Religion in New England in 1740," suggested to Joseph Tracy the preparation of a history of that revival. His design was admirably executed. Subordinate attention was given by him to the progress of the revival in other sections of the country and in Great Britain, but in the main his *Great Awakening* is an exhaustive history of the revival proper in New England. It gives extended quotations from the personal narratives of many promoters of the revival which were written in 1743 and 1744 for Prince's *Christian History*.

Approaching my task almost three-fourths of a century after Tracy, I find myself more in sympathy than was common in Tracy's day with the catholicity of Whitefield and with the democratic tendencies of the revival which were so largely responsible for the destruction of the ecclesiastical system of New England. Tracy wrote with the purpose of encouraging a similar quickening in his own time but wished to avoid resort to measures which he imagined to be harmful. I find my purpose not in the advocacy of a program but in the attempt to demonstrate that the religious energies liberated by the Great Awakening were transformed into forces, social, humanitarian, educational, and political, which have been of almost incalculable importance in the making of the American people.

This study, much briefer than Tracy's, will make only such reference to the revival in New England as is demanded for understanding the movement in the Middle Colonies. The statement of the relation of the revival in the Middle Colonies to its extension southward will not be so abbreviated, because that relation was very close, and because there is no account of the revival in the South like that of Tracy for New England.

I made a journey from Boston, Massachusetts, to Charleston, South Carolina, visiting most of the libraries which possess important collections of colonial newspapers. I gathered a mass of material on the moral and religious conditions of the colonies and the progress of the Great Awakening. Though everywhere courteously received, I feel myself under special obligation to the gentlemen in charge of the splendid collections of the Massachusetts Historical Society. In the notes a number of references to the newspapers, a neglected source material, will be found.

I have also visited libraries at New York, New Brunswick, Princeton, Trenton, and Philadelphia. Special mention must be made of some among the many visited. At the library of Union Theological Seminary I was given kindly assistance and access to rare books of the eighteenth century. At the Sage Library, New Brunswick, I found useful material on the relation of the Dutch church to the revival. At the Princeton Theological Library I was given access to the incomparable Sprague Collection. At Trenton the permanent clerk of the presbytery of New Brunswick, Rev. George H. Ingram, permitted me to inspect the manuscript records of that body and kindly presented me with a typewritten copy of the first record book. He was then writing a history of the presbytery of New Brunswick for the *Presbyterian Historical Review*. At Philadelphia my indebtedness among a number of libraries is greatest to that of the Presbyterian Historical Society. Here the extensive collection of Tennent papers, mostly manuscript sermons of Gilbert Tennent, was put at my disposal, as were also the records of the Second Presbyterian Church of Philadelphia and many old books and pamphlets not found elsewhere.

Source materials other than those mentioned in the statement of my obligations are the journals of Whitefield and Brainerd, Prince's *Christian History*, the *Records of the Presbyterian Church*, and many excerpts from eighteenth-century documents which are incorporated in the histories of churches, presbyteries, and denominations and in the biographies of men who were concerned in the movement. The *Ecclesiastical Records of the State of New York* are a mine of information upon the progress of revivalism in New York and New Jersey and to some extent in Pennsylvania.

The story of Pietism in Pennsylvania is based principally upon the extensive researches of Sachse and serves as an introduction to the more important phases of the revival, the story of which follows. Chapters ii to viii and the greater part of chapter ix are based on original material. So far as chapter ix deals with denominations other than the Presbyterian and Dutch Reformed it is based for the most part on denominational histories, secondary sources, though Edwards' *Material* may very properly be regarded as original. This part of chapter ix simply fills out the story and shows the remarkable parallelism in the results of the Great Awakening in the various denominations. The final chapter sums up a number of the distinguishing marks of the evangelical revival.

CONTENTS

CHAPTER I

INTRODUCTION, AND PIETISM IN PENNSYLVANIA

In the middle of the eighteenth century a tidal wave of religious fervor and reforming zeal swept over the British colonies in America. When this wave of emotionalism had passed, when the extraordinary in Christian experience and activity had given place to the ordinary, the friends of the revival, and after them their sons and sons' sons, called it the Great Awakening.

The term "Great Awakening," however, is not employed in this study in a restricted sense as applying only to the religious excitement of 1740, or even to the series of widely extended and closely related revivals among which that of 1740 was the most remarkable. The name is used as an appropriate designation of the whole evangelical quickening in the colonies. This change in the attitude of the people toward religion, by which after a period of decay it became a power in the lives of thousands, had numerous and widely separated beginnings very early in the century. Among these beginnings the most important were the revival of Pietism among the Germans of Pennsylvania, the rise of a radical evangelism among the Dutch of New Jersey, a similar revival among the English-speaking Presbyterians of the Middle Colonies, and, following these, the remarkable outburst of old-time Puritan feeling among the Congregationalists of New England. Though this intercolonial and interdenominational quickening rose at times to astonishing heights of excitement, these seasons were but passing manifestations of an abiding movement. It was still powerful in parts of the country at the breaking out of the Revolutionary War.

Though the Great Awakening, conceived of as a long-sustained movement, was professedly unsectarian, and its promoters were not concerned with the ecclesiastical affiliations of the religiously awakened, yet the denominations which heartily accepted its principles became strong and popular. The degree of their acceptance of these evangelistic ideals was the measure of their ultimate numerical strength. This building up of large bodies of aggressive religionists which possessed no special privileges and opposed the union of church and state contributed greatly to a social and political revolution. However vivid to the imaginations of New Lights and New Sides[1] were heaven and hell, they excelled their more conservative brethren in determined pursuit of practical aims. Their awakened sympathy established orphanages and other institutions for social betterment. They gave new life to missions. In that time there were no other founders of schools like them. When a conservative majority in a colony held the evangelical minority in unwilling restraint, relief was found in emigration, and whole churches of the discontented moved beyond the jurisdiction of the persecuting government. Thus the Great Awakening was not wave on wave of excitement which, having passed, left no trace upon the placid waters. It was a powerful ferment which was destined to revolutionize colonial society. As an intercolonial movement it was the beginning of a unifying process which was carried still farther by common effort in the French and Indian War and to political union by the Revolutionary War.

Not only was the Great Awakening an intercolonial movement; it was part of a larger awakening within the whole British Empire which may very properly be called the Methodist Revival. Waves of influence crossed the Atlantic in both directions. The remarkable revival which began in 1734 at Northampton under the preaching of Jonathan Edwards, already mentioned as one of the beginnings of the Great Awakening, was reported in Great Britain, first by the letters of American correspondents, and afterward by the publication in 1737 of Edwards' *Narrative of Surprising Conversions*.[2] Dissenters and conformists were stirred by its reading,[3] and it was influential in the spread of the revival spirit in the homelands.[4] Pious colonists in turn became expectant and hopeful

[1] The former term was employed in New England and was frequently applied to the radical supporters of the revival; the latter term was employed in the Middle Colonies, but there it was applied to the evangelical party in the Presbyterian Church.

[2] Rev. W. Williams, of Hatfield, wrote a letter to Dr. Colman, of Boston, on the "Remarkable Success of the Gospel" in Hampshire county, dated April 28, 1735, which was published in the *New England Weekly Journal*, May 12, 1735. Colman forwarded this and other accounts to his correspondents, Drs. Watts and Guyse, of London. They asked for a fuller statement, which request Edwards received in a letter written by Colman to Williams. The narrative was dated November 6, 1736, and was published in London in 1737. The Boston *Gazette*, December 20, 1736, advertises that "*An Account of the late wonderful Work of God* by Rev. Jonathan, Edwards is JUST PUBLISHED." This is the narrative of November 6, 1736, abridged by Dr. Colman. The same paper, December 11, 1738, advertised Edwards' *Surprising Work of God*. This was the unabridged narrative of 1736. The statement in Dwight's *Edwards*, Vol. I of Edwards' Works, pp. 137–40, is not accurate.

[3] Hoskins, "German Influence," *Princeton Theological Review*, 1907.

[4] Tyerman's *Wesley*, I, 220; Macpherson, *A History of the Church in Scotland*, p. 324.

when the beginnings of a religious quickening in England were reported to them. Readers of the colonial newspapers[1] in January, 1738, found astonishing accounts of the preaching in the preceding October of a young deacon of the Church of England, Whitefield by name, a member of John Wesley's student club, derisively called the Methodists. Later the colonial papers[2] copied from their London exchanges almost incredible stories of the throngs which crowded around the young orator, now become a field preacher. When, therefore, he arrived at Lewes, Delaware, on October 30, 1739, interest in the great evangelist was already raised to the highest pitch. From that day George Whitefield, the English Methodist, was the chief figure in the Great Awakening in the American colonies. For nearly a decade there was constant interchange of reports by both friends and enemies of the revival. English and Scotch tracts and sermons were republished by enterprising printers from Charleston to Boston, and colonial publications reappeared in Glasgow and London.

But the Great Awakening was not only part of the larger Methodist Revival, a movement within the British Empire; it was part of an international evangelical revival which among the Protestants of Germany was known as the pietistic movement.[3] In this world movement emphasis was not put upon distinctive names, formal creeds, the claims of this or that system of church polity, or upon the efficacy of merely external rites. Its fundamental ideas were vital piety, the mystic union of the believer with God, the enthronement of emotion upon its rightful seat, and a thoroughgoing reformation of morals.

Spener, of Frankfort, was the founder of Pietism.[4] Beginning in 1670 he established *collegia pietatis*, or private devotional societies,

---

[1] *American Weekly Mercury*, January 24, 1738, and other papers.

[2] Boston *Gazette*, June 25, 1739, and many other papers.

[3] *Christian History* for 1744, pp. 262–84. This weekly paper, edited by T. Prince, Jr., was the first religious periodical published in the colonies. Similar weekly histories of religion had recently been established in London by Whitefield and in Glasgow by McLaurin. These papers illustrate the international character of the revival, in the promotion of which they were established. The *Christian History* prints an account of the revival in Germany, which account was the preface to the English edition of 1705 of Francke's *Pietatas Hallensis*. Cotton Mather had previously corresponded with Francke and contributed to his work. They exchanged books. Knowledge of the revival in Germany must have awakened the desire for revival in New England and may have contributed to the revival of 1734. On Mather see Hoskins, pp. 210, 225.

[4] The term "Pietism" is employed here in the sense of Riggenbach as a reaction of practical faith from barren orthodoxy, not as a vague term including various speculative and mystical phenomena. Yet there is an undoubted relation between the Labadists, Quakers, Quietists, and Pietists. Kaufmann, "Latitudinarianism and Pietism," in *Cambridge Modern History*, V, 753 ff.

within the churches, through which he hoped to leaven the whole lump. In these societies the Bible was enthusiastically studied, and the spiritual priesthood of laymen was exercised. Spener advocated gentleness in the intercourse of Lutherans and the Reformed and was called to Berlin by the king of Prussia as a pacificator. Under his influence the new University of Halle was manned with professors of pietistic sentiment. Halle accordingly became the center of evangelism in Germany. Presently the Lutheran communion was divided into two parties. The minority held to Pietism, though repudiating every charge of separation and heresy. The majority charged that the establishment of a church within the church inevitably paved the way to separation, and that the boasted catholicism of the Pietists but opened the door to heresy, enthusiasm, and chiliastic reveries.[1]

Spener died in 1705, but already Francke had succeeded him as a vigorous leader of the movement. It was Francke who established the famous orphan house at Halle with its affiliated schools and various institutions for the propagation of this warm type of religion. Under his direction Pietism continued to exercise a wholesome influence upon the Lutheran Church, for it was a protest against dogmatism and formalism. Yet it was narrow in its tendency to define conversion in the terms of a single type. This narrowness was transmitted to the Methodist Revival.

The course of Pietism in the Lutheran Church of Germany may be dismissed with this brief characterization, but a word is demanded concerning the influence of the revival upon the various religious bodies the members of which swarmed to the New World and here participated in the Great Awakening. The Reformed as well as the Lutherans of the Palatinate, from which principality the main emigration was made from Germany to Pennsylvania, were under strong pietistic influences. But none responded more quickly to the new touch of life than the so-called "Sectarian" bodies. The pietistic propaganda was a boon to them, for they too stood for experimental religion and the universal priesthood of believers. In addition to these principles, held in common with the revivalists of the established churches, they more or less generally held such doctrines as the separation of church and state, non-resistance, prohibition of oaths, plainness of dress, the love feast, the kiss of charity, and foot-washing.[2]

Of these Sectarians, aroused by the revival to activity, the most numerous connection was that of the Mennonites, the representatives

---

[1] Mirbt, "Pietism," in *New Schaff-Herzog Rel. Enc.*, Vol. IX.

[2] Kuhns, *The German and Swiss Settlements of Colonial Pennsylvania*, p. 173.

of the Anabaptists of the Reformation. The Schwenkfelders were another survival of the same period. More important than the Schwenkfelders, but like them insignificant in numbers, were the Dunkers, or German Baptist Brethren.[1] Though the spirit of Pietism was opposed to the organization of new sects, this brotherhood was none the less the fruit of the revival. The Moravians illustrated the opposite and prevailing tendency of the revival, the tendency to union and affiliation with all denominations. The Unitas Fratrum, the ancient Moravian Church, uprooted from its ancestral home, was reorganized by Count Zinzendorf in Germany and became beyond any other sect the very embodiment of Pietism. Moravianism was a wonderful system with its classes and discipline, with its hierarchy and co-operative business enterprises, with its orphanages and schools, with its vent for emotion and recreation in strangely appealing music, and above all with its truly heroic prosecution of foreign missions.[2]

Again the general international character of the whole religious movement can be seen from the relation between the German reformers and the men of England whom the new spirit was beginning to move. John Wesley was converted through the instrumentality of Peter Boehler, the Moravian. The Methodist societies in the Church of England adopted many features of Moravianism. Indeed the members of that brotherhood were pre-eminently the mediators of German Pietism to the revivalists of England. Moreover, George Whitefield, the chief apostle of the Great Awakening, was influenced profoundly by Pietism. In the story of his youth Whitefield tells of his first meeting with Charles Wesley.[3] Whitefield was then a young Pembroke College student, shy but thirsting for spiritual friendship. Wesley understood his need and put into his hands Francke's treatise, the *Fear of Man*. This was Whitefield's introduction to the German Pietist whose orphan house at Halle was the model of his own in Georgia, and to whose example he frequently appealed. Whitefield's reading was not in systems of doctrine[4] but in devotional books, pietistical and mystical, sometimes passionate in their portrayal of the struggles of the tempted. Ardent and imaginative as he was by nature, he experienced the very struggles of which he read, even suffering the torments of the damned. His surrender to these suggestions in such extreme fashion he afterward regarded as yielding to

[1] Brumbaugh, *A History of the German Baptist Brethren*, p. 12.

[2] *Pennsylvania Gazette*, February 24, 1743.

[3] Whitefield, *Brief Account*, pp. 19, 20.

[4] Whitefield, *A Letter . . . . in Answer to . . . . Querists*, p. 61.

the temptations of Satan.   But these struggles were very real to him
and threw him into serious illness.   At last his cry for relief was heard.
Then his exaltation of spirit even exceeded the measure of his former
distress.   He was the first of the band of Methodists to pass through
what the Moravians called "holy mourning" to its happy issue in
assurance.[1]

The influence of Pietism upon Whitefield did not end with his conversion.   There are frequent references in his journals to pietistic literature.[2]   The native tendency of his mind to eschew plodding logical
processes and to leap at one bound to conclusions was encouraged by
the mystical books which he read and by his intercourse with the Moravians.   Deep impressions and sudden impulses were followed as inspira-
tions of the divine Spirit, but if they proved harmful and erroneous they
were afterward attributed to Satan.   It was this that Jonathan Edwards
criticized in friendly conversation with Whitefield, and it was this that
Charles Chauncy openly denounced as Quakerish and Jesuitical superstition.[3]   But impulses and impressions were incidental; from Pietism
the evangelist had learned that Christianity is a life, not a creed; the
glow and warmth of that life he had come to feel himself.

But Pietism had another connection with the religious movement
which is to be traced in these chapters, more direct, if less potent, than
that indicated by its effects upon the Wesleys, Whitefield, and other
Methodist leaders, for Pietists came in great numbers to the Middle
Colonies, and their influence ultimately determined the dominant character of the colonial German population.   In 1683, two years after
William Penn obtained his charter, the first body of German emigrants
arrived in Philadelphia and soon afterward founded Germantown.   They
were attracted by the proposals of Penn's *Holy Experiment*.   The company was composed of Mennonites and German Quakers.[4]

The Mennonites were followed in 1694 by a strange body of mystics,
forty in number, including university men of varied learning.   First of
all these mystics were Pietists, but they were also chiliasts.[5]   It is remark-

[1] Whitefield, *Brief Account*, pp. 31, 40.   Whitefield was converted in 1735 and
Wesley in 1738; that is, in those years they passed through the emotional experiences
which they accounted their conversions.

[2] Whitefield's *Journals* for January 6, 9, and March 26, 1738; September 15,
1739, etc.

[3] Hoskins, *op. cit.*, p. 223; Dwight, *op. cit.*, p. 147; Chauncy, *Seasonable Thoughts*,
p. 173.

[4] Sachse, *German Pietists*, p. 4.   [5] *Ibid.*, pp. 37, 38, 80, 129, 130.

able that every revival of religion revives too the belief of the early Christians in the speedy return of the Lord. This body was sometimes called the Order of the Woman in the Wilderness, for were its members not carried over the sea by the "wings of the great eagle," and did they not flee into the wilderness, where God, as they imagined, had prepared a place for them?[1] Here they would wait for the harbinger of the millennium soon to dawn upon the world, according to the calculations of their astronomers and astrologists. They were orthodox Lutherans, but they held in addition to the usual articles of faith these esoteric doctrines. Science and pseudo-science were strangely commingled, for they practiced medicine and manufactured amulets, studied botany and employed the divining rod to determine the location of springs of water.[2]

In contrast with the coming of this little band of enthusiasts there was in 1709 the arrival of a horde of destitute Palatines. Most of them were brought to the province of New York by the English government. A few of those who first settled in New York made their way down the Susquehanna River and finally reached the more hospitable province of Pennsylvania. In 1717 the immigration of Palatines direct to Pennsylvania was suddenly swelled by the coming of six or seven thousand. They were Reformed and Lutherans in approximately equal numbers, many of both communions holding pietistic views. They were driven from the fatherland by religious persecution and economic distress.[3]

Not all these Germans who year by year sought refuge in the New World were members of the two leading churches. Little companies of Sectarians arrived from time to time. In 1719 the Dunkers came. There were only twenty families, and these scattered to obtain suitable lands. Ten years later their founder, Alexander Mack, brought a large company to Germantown. The Dunkers were followed by the Schwenkfelders in 1734, and that year a few Moravian evangelists arrived. Thus the several denominations which had been stirred by the new evangel in the fatherland, and which were to be active in pious endeavor in the New World, were now planted in Pennsylvania, and some of them were also represented in New York and New Jersey.[4]

America was at first a disappointing refuge to these German immigrants. The hard conditions on the frontier, the exhausting labor of

[1] Rev. 12:1–6, 13–17; 20:4.   [2] Sachse, *op. cit.*, pp. 62, 112, 120.

[3] *Ecclesiastical Records of the State of New York*, p. 1712.

[4] Brumbaugh, *op. cit.*, p. 49. It is estimated that up to 1739 there had been a German emigration to Pennsylvania of thirty to thirty-five thousand. Kuhns, *op. cit.*, pp. 55, 57.

clearing the forests, the isolation of life, the breaking of former ties, the lack of encouragement from coreligionists—all these things had a benumbing effect upon the German immigrants, much to the detriment of their religious and intellectual well-being. Some, who had suffered the spoiling of their goods for sake of conscience in the Old World, seemed to lose their religion in the New World. They saw their children growing up in ignorance. They were perplexed by the religious confusion, for there were many sects among the Germans besides those mentioned, and some of them held views dangerous to society. The members of churches maintained by the state in the fatherland were unaccustomed to voluntary support of the gospel. Even the Sectarians were baffled for the time being. Such were the conditions in the early years when the material foundation was being laid.[1]

The prospect was discouraging, but the event proved that these plodding Germans had chosen the best lands and thus had the basis for material prosperity, while the leaven of Pietism in time gave character to the whole society. Among them mystical and pietistic leaders worked effectively. The forty mystics mentioned as coming to Pennsylvania in 1694 sought to meet the religious needs of the German colonists. Though these mystics had buried themselves in the western wilderness, their tabernacle was but three miles from Germantown. Children were received to be educated by them, and all who studied at the tabernacle were deeply imbued with the spirit of Pietism. This was the first charitable institution in Pennsylvania. Kelpius, the leader of the band, professing love for all denominations, sought to unite the Germans in one church. He was held in great veneration, but he died early, and even before his death the symbolical number of forty was broken by withdrawals.[2]

The associates of Kelpius were highly individualistic in their ideas and practices. Koster observed the Seventh-day as a day of sacred rest and immersed his converts from Quakerism when they insisted on following scriptural precedent. Others he led back to the Church of England. Thus the Baptists and Episcopalians were indebted to this Lutheran minister whose chief work was among the German people.[3] The Falkner brothers, Daniel and Justus, also members of the order, gave years of missionary service to their fellow Lutherans. They were itinerant

---

[1] Sachse, *German Sectarians*, pp. 50–52.   [2] Kuhns, *op. cit.*, p. 86.

[3] Sachse, *The German Pietists*, pp. 274, 277, 286; Morgan Edwards, *Material*, p. 45; Vedder, *A History of the Baptists in the Middle States*, p. 64; McConnell, *History of the American Episcopal Church*, pp. 80, 81.

pastors for a great part of New York and New Jersey.   Others of the band served as physicians and lay workers.   At last the tabernacle was deserted.   Only a solitary recluse, here and there, was left of the company that were called "Pietists" in distinction from all others.   Whitefield tells of an interview with the hermit Matthai, the successor of Kelpius.   Some members of the order lived even until the arrival of Muhlenberg, himself a Pietist from Halle, who was sent by Francke's orphanage as a missionary to America.[1]

Notwithstanding the efforts of these missionaries of pietistic sentiment and of others of conservative opinion violently opposed to Pietism, the religious destitution was great among the Lutherans and still greater among the Reformed.   There was difficulty in obtaining regularly ordained and university-trained ministers, but the Sectarians, requiring only that education which comes from the exercise of gifts, often developed religious leaders of remarkable power.   Furthermore, they were self-supporting.   For this reason the Mennonites, and notably the Dunkers, were far more active and successful than the more numerous Lutherans and Reformed.   Peter Becker, the leader of the first company of Dunkers, was discouraged by the separation of his people to obtain homes, but his spirit was stirred by a Mennonite revival in Germantown in 1722.   The following year he organized a little church of the German Baptist Brethren.   There were other revivals under Dunker patronage, though the principal evangelist was a mystic, Beissel, not of their number.[2]

Beissel had come to America intending to join the mystics on the Wissahickon, but finding the tabernacle deserted he became a recluse like some of the surviving members of the order.   He was a man of genius.   He had intercourse with the solitary Pietists, with the Labadists of Maryland, and with Seventh-day Baptists.   In 1723 he actually joined the Dunkers, but he brought with him an eclectic assortment of ideas and practices borrowed from all with whom he had had relations. The result was a schism among the brethren.   Finally Beissel established the famous communistic institution at Ephrata.[3]

Though the Dunkers were greatly weakened by constant defection to their brethren who kept the Seventh-day, they did not lose the evangelistic spirit.   There was special evidence of this after Alexander Mack, founder of the sect, came to Pennsylvania, seeking rest from wanderings

---

[1] Sachse, *The German Pietists*, pp. 299–386, 402; Whitefield, *Journal*, No. 5, p. 48.

[2] Sachse, *The German Pietists*, pp. 52, 78.

[3] *Ibid.*, p. 104.

and persecutions in the Old World.   As a result of frequent revivals a number of churches were organized.   The converts were taken, of course, from the neglected Lutheran and Reformed population.   When Zinzendorf called the first Pennsylvania synod, of which an account will be given in a later chapter, the Dunkers were able to send their delegation to the united council of the German churches as representing a body of earnest religionists of very considerable strength.   In principles the German Baptist Brethren were like the Quakers, but they retained a propagating zeal which the Quakers were fast losing.[1]

Thus while the Great Awakening was part of the contemporaneous Methodist Revival and part of a world movement which had begun in Germany and was known on the Continent as Pietism, so the revival of Pietism among the Germans of the Middle Colonies was one of the several beginnings of the Great Awakening.   This separate stream of emotional religion has been traced in this chapter only to its junction in 1739 with other streams of like nature.   The operations of Zinzendorf, the Moravian, Muhlenberg, the Lutheran, and Schlatter, the organizer of the German Reformed Church, belonging to a later period, will be described in their appropriate connections.   Throughout the eighteenth century the Germans of Pennsylvania were peculiarly subject to religious excitement.[2]   The pietistic sentiments of early and influential settlers and the labors of itinerant evangelists kept alive warm religious feeling.   Pietism in its radical individualism brought to the New World men fantastically diverse from each other.   Yet in spite of superficial differences, as true Pietists, they were sympathetic with all Christians and held as a fundamental principle that Christianity in its essence is the life of God in the soul of man.

[1] Brumbaugh, *op. cit.*, pp. 165, 198.

[2] Kuhns, *op. cit.*, p. 155.

CHAPTER II

FRELINGHUYSEN, AND THE BEGINNING OF THE REVIVAL AMONG THE DUTCH REFORMED

A second distinct source of the Great Awakening is associated with a family name honored in the annals of New Jersey, that of Frelinghuysen. The comparative affluence of the Dutch in New York and New Jersey was very different in the first half of the eighteenth century from the almost servile station of the Germans in Pennsylvania and adjoining colonies. The Germans were more acted upon than acting in the general religious quickening, at least before the landing of Count Zinzendorf upon our shores. The reformation throughout the country did not have its one common origin among these recent comers. It did not spread from them to the Dutch, Scotch-Irish, and New Englanders in the Middle Colonies. The revival in the Dutch Reformed Church was a separate movement in its early stages. Yet the originator of this movement, Domine Frelinghuysen, was not a Hollander, and the Dutch language was not his native tongue. He was a German and in the fatherland had come under pietistic influence. So thoroughly was he the soul of the evangelical revival among the Dutch until the coming of Whitefield that the account of the movement up to that time is the story of his life. These biographical details are nevertheless important, for their main outline is strangely parallel with the course of the revival everywhere else. The reformation within the Dutch Reformed Church was a notable movement, but the direct influence of this revival upon the Scotch-Irish Presbyterians was so powerful and through them the indirect influence upon the general movement was so pronounced that some have declared that the actual beginning of the Great Awakening was in those stirring meetings in log churches and barns on the frontier of New Jersey. This is claiming too much. A more accurate statement is that the Dutch revival was the second of the distinct sources of the Great Awakening in the Middle Colonies and more important for the general movement than the revival among the Germans.

The "frontier of New Jersey"—what was the social and ecclesiastical background of Frelinghuysen's labors? The Valley of the Raritan had been described to the multiplying Dutch of the Hudson Valley about the middle of the seventeenth century as "the pleasantest country that man can behold."[1]   A degree of persecution in the province of New York was an added incentive to the westward movement.   The sturdy Dutch farmers of New Jersey did not have the religious and educational advantages of New England frontiersmen, but they were like them in this, that as the New Englanders of each succeeding generation lost something of the religious devotion and Old World culture of their fathers, so too the Dutchmen of the Middle Colonies had lapsed from what the Hollanders of the seventeenth century had been.[2]   These frontiersmen particularly were rough and boorish; the moral delinquencies of a primitive peasantry were found among them.[3]   Nevertheless the Dutch settlers of the Raritan were in a way religious—in quite the same way as other men of their blood in both provinces.[4]   In name their religion was that long before defined by the synod of Dordrecht; in fact it was an instinctive attachment to their Dutch nationality.   The first article of their real creed was therefore veneration for their language.   The second article was the preservation of the dependence of their churches on the classis of Amsterdam[5] as the ghost of their former political dependence.   They were strenuous supporters of orthodoxy, but orthodoxy to them was doing every least thing in the same way in which it had always been done.[6] Two venerable rites[7] were in their minds the sum of religious duty and privilege.   Of spiritual struggles they knew nothing.   There was no demand upon the emotional nature and little upon conduct except in a superficial conformity to certain universally accepted maxims of morality.

A generation passed after the beginning of the settlement in 1684 before the Dutch of the Raritan felt able to call a pastor.[8]   Then as a united congregation they sent a call through Domine Freeman, of Long Island, to Holland.[9]   He committed the trust to a member of the evangelical party, which, though containing great lights, was in the minority in

---

[1] Messler, *Memorial Sermons*, p. 159.

[2] Messler, *The Hollander in New Jersey*, p. 4;   *Memorial Sermons*, p. 24.

[3] Frelinghuysen, *Sermons*, pp. 65, 88, 223, 224.

[4] Messler, *Memorial Sermons*, p. 24.

[5] The classis of the Reformed Church corresponds to the presbytery of the Presbyterian.   The jurisdiction of this one classis over the Dutch churches, established in foreign parts, grew out of the custom of the trading companies to apply to the classis of Amsterdam to appoint chaplains and pastors for their oversea factories and settlements.

[6] *Ecclesiastical Records of the State of New York*, pp. 2198, 2208.

[7] Baptism and Lord's Supper.

[8] Messler, *Memorial Sermons*, p. 204.   [9] *Ibid.*, pp. 163, 166.

Holland as in Germany. The choice fell upon a young man of enterprise and piety, Theodorus J. Frelinghuysen, who had already made a name for himself, but who welcomed the opportunity, according to the report of the captain of the ship on which he sailed, of exercising his freedom from restraint in the New World by leading a reformation such as the majority of the ministers in Holland opposed.[1] It was said that he hoped to bring over others of his fraternity. Landing at New York in January, 1720, he was invited to preach in the city.[2] His first sermon was like the proclamation of a new gospel, so animated was his plea for a religion of power. Formalists like Domine Boel, junior pastor of the Dutch Reformed Church, were offended and sharply rebuked the apostle of revivalism, who had thus no sooner set foot on American soil than he aroused the opposition of men in high place. Soon the university graduate was making the circuit of his four frontier churches, traveling great distances between the scattered settlements, fording streams, and picking his way through forests. The change was quite as great for his parishioners as for their pastor. Formerly a neighboring minister had made them an occasional visit for the administration of the ordinances, but their usual dependence had been upon the halting reading of a *voorleser*.[3] Now they had a pastor, and with him came a teacher, for Dutch churches, like the German Reformed, aimed to establish schools in connection with their churches.

Never had the people of the Raritan seen such earnestness, such passion, in the pulpit. Frelinghuysen defined life in terms of which they had never dreamed. The doctrines he taught were so new that they seemed a departure from the Dutch Reformed teachings.[4] He declared that God hates the outward performance of religious duties apart from a suitable frame of mind.[5] The pastor described regeneration as such a thoroughgoing conversion, such a crisis in the believer's experience,[6] that almost none of his hearers dared claim that they had been converted.[7] The result was that even his elders and deacons who sat with him at the table forbore to commune.[8]

[1] The captain denied the story in the form reported by the Boels. *Eccl. Rec. of New York*, pp. 2182, 2260, 2333, 2386.

[2] *Ibid.*, p. 2259.

[3] The *voorlesers* corresponded to the early readers in Scotch churches. See "Sum of the First Book of Discipline" in *Confessions of Faith*, p. 56.

[4] *Eccl. Rec. of New York*, p. 2197.

[5] Frelinghuysen, *op. cit.*, p. 26.   [7] *Eccl. Rec. of New York*, pp. 2250, 2272.

[6] *Ibid.*, pp. 48, 115.   [8] *Ibid.*, pp. 2255, 2289.

The younger and poorer people were disposed to accept this teaching as true. Frelinghuysen maintained that in every age it is just such that accept the gospel.[1] The well-to-do and the former leaders in the settlements were outraged by such teachings.[2] They rushed to New York for advice.[3] Domine Boel set forth baptismal regeneration,[4] while according to Frelinghuysen a crisis without reference to a ceremony was necessary. That a stage of this crisis might border upon despair was abhorrent doctrine to Boel.[5] The claim that a minister might examine another person upon his spiritual attainments, and upon the basis of such examination give his judgment as to his conversion, was to Boel unqualified heresy.[6] The new emphasis upon the divine life in the soul and upon the leading of the Spirit was in Boel's estimation Quaker doctrine.[7] Boel was right in this; it is extraordinary that the Quakers did not themselves recognize the Great Awakening as a revival of their own doctrine. The disaffected returned to their homes, reporting upon the authority of the New York divine that Frelinghuysen was a schismatic and heretic.

Thereupon the domine in defense published three sermons which contained his teaching upon the controverted points. Domine Bartholf, who had organized some, if not all, of the churches in the Raritan Valley, and Freeman, who had introduced Frelinghuysen to them, united in a recommendation. They judged the sermons not only "learned, well digested, and thrilling" but "highly sound and scriptural."[8] Boel accepted the challenge so far as to preach in his own pulpit in opposition to the teaching of these sermons.[9] He visited the disaffected on the Raritan and organized them for resistance.[10] The majority of the North Branch congregation signed a paper notifying the heretical domine that their meeting-house was built only for orthodox worship.[11] One prominent member who, like many others, refused to pay his subscription was compelled to pay by civil action.[12] The disaffected also appealed to the courts, but without success.[13] They even besought the governor to remove the heretic;[14] it was in vain.

---

[1] *Eccl. Rec. of New York*, p. 354.

[2] *Ibid.*, pp. 2201, 2258, 2264.

[3] *Ibid.*, p. 2266.

[4] *Ibid.*, p. 2250.

[5] *Ibid.*, p. 2249.

[6] *Ibid.*, pp. 2252, 2253, 2260.

[7] *Ibid.*, p. 2179.

[8] *Ibid.*, p. 2265.

[9] *Ibid.*, pp. 2272, 2328.

[10] *Ibid.*, p. 2264.

[11] *Ibid.*, p. 2210.

[12] *Ibid.*, p. 2387.

[13] Frelinghuysen, *op. cit.*, p. 353.

[14] *Ibid.*, pp. 29, 31.

Frelinghuysen had advocated in his sermons the power of the keys, the power of discipline in the hands of the consistory,[1] even to the extent of excommunication of the disaffected.[2] After long delay four of the leaders were put under the ban.[3] They represented the wealth and, according to their own account, the majority of the membership of the several congregations. Thus the reward of three years' toil was the disruption of his churches. In the next two years the disaffected gathered the evidence against the pastor, and Lawyer Boel, brother of the domine of the same name, wove it together with considerable skill.[4] This famous *Complaint*, making a printed book of two hundred and forty-six pages, published in 1725, is alone sufficient to gain for the domine the sympathy of the fair-minded. On every page what is now the usual order of things is treated as the unheard-of and monstrous. The defenders of Frelinghuysen among the pastors shared in the castigation given the reformer. Thereupon Freeman published a defense[5] and Van Santvoord a dialogue[6] in the interest of Frelinghuysen and evangelical doctrine. The *Complaint*, on the other hand, was sent overseas to the classis of Amsterdam, with a letter of approval signed by a number of pastors.[7] Thus the division which began on the frontier now divided the Dutch pastors of the two provinces into hostile camps.

Frelinghuysen did not believe that the lack of success in his early ministry was anything but the temporary rebuff which every faithful minister must expect in an age when evangelical doctrine had become so obsolete as to be mistaken for heresy. He denounced the sins rife in the valley with such stinging directness that a reformation in morals was slowly effected. He presented Christianity as a force that revolutionizes the conduct of the believer. The domine was a university-extension department, stimulating, wherever he went, the intellectual life of the people. He had the genius to seize upon young men of exceptional ability and charge them with something of his own force. The

---

[1] *Eccl. Rec. of New York*, pp. 2383, 2403; Talmage, *A Sermon*, p. 19. A consistory was composed of pastor, elders, and deacons, one half of the lay membership retiring each year. The new members were elected by the old consistory. This is pure presbyterian government, in that the rulers are not elected by the people. See "Westminster Directory" in *Confessions of Faith*, p. 487.

[2] Frelinghuysen, *op. cit.*, p. 82.   [4] *Ibid.*, p. 2244.

[3] *Eccl. Rec. of New York*, pp. 2201, 2206, 2212, 2291.   [5] *Ibid.*, p. 2307.

[6] Van Santvoord was pastor on Staten Island. *Eccl. Rec. of New York*, p. 2349.

[7] *Ibid.*, p. 2309.

elders and deacons were converted one after another, until the last deacon made his new confession in 1725.[1]   The members of the four churches were becoming a "very different people."   The congregations of the domine increased, and there were numerous conversions among people who were not before upon the roll of the churches.   In some years, particularly in 1726, the ingathering was so great proportionately as to give a foregleam of the time when Whitefield should come flaming through the country.   The subjects of the revival had all experienced such a conversion as had never before been insisted upon in these provinces—a severe spiritual conflict ending in a passionate determination to make the attainment of their highest moral ideals the dominating purpose of their lives.

The revival spirit was not confined to the four churches on the Raritan.   Frelinghuysen was invited by pastors to visit other places. Lawyer Boel asked in irony, "Why does he not stay with those congregations whose minister he is and first seek out the many unconverted souls that are there, instead of depriving them of spiritual food by going so often to other places?"[2]   In two instances he intruded on the fields of other pastors.[3]   Though goaded to this by the publication of pamphlets against him charging heresy,[4] and by constant intrusion upon his own field,[5] this action was inconsistent with his reiterated complaint against these pastors for this same offense.   Perhaps in his own mind intrusion was sometimes justifiable where shepherds were hirelings,[6] but reprehensible where pastors faithfully preached the gospel.   At any rate, by methods upon occasion disorderly but in general orderly, the revival was spreading from the Raritan Valley to other parts.   At the same time pastors of other churches who opposed the revival kept alive the opposition in the valley.

The revival begun by Frelinghuysen also spread to newly organized Presbyterian churches in the valley.   In 1726 there were English-speaking dissenters scattered through the region who were like "sheep gone astray."[7]   Some of the people therefore called a young Presbyterian licentiate, and he was ordained at New Brunswick in the autumn of that year.[8]   His name was Gilbert Tennent, who later became known on both sides of the ocean as the foremost Presbyterian promoter of the

---

[1] *Eccl. Rec. of New York*, pp. 2288, 2289, 2387.   [2] *Ibid.*, p. 2275.

[3] Of Morgan and Coens.   *Ibid.*, p. 2466.

[4] *Ibid.*, p. 2306.

[5] Frelinghuysen, *op. cit.*, p. 355.

[6] *Eccl. Rec. of New York*, p. 2304.   [7] *Ibid.*, p. 2557.

[8] Webster, *A History of the Presbyterian Church*, p. 387.

Great Awakening. The Dutch subscribed to his salary to encourage the less numerous English.[1] Even some of the enemies of Frelinghuysen did so at first.[2] The domine gave him the use of his meeting-houses and of barns of adherents in which he was himself accustomed to preach. After a time the two men entered upon exceedingly cordial relations, and the direct and pungent method of preaching which gave offense to the more worldly members of the Dutch churches was also adopted by the younger minister.[3] Sometimes they held joint services, one speaking in Dutch and the other in English. This was shocking to the Dutch complainants, and to them it was even sacrilege when the domine joined with the "dissenter," as they called him, in the celebration of the Lord's Supper.[4]

Henceforth one of the chief complaints against the domine was his encouragement of Tennent. It was represented that the introduction of the English language into Dutch churches was a violation of church order. It was reported to the classis that this dissenter, like Frelinghuysen, held pietistic views.[5] In reply to inquiries the domine maintained that the churches of Scotland and the Netherlands were sister Reformed churches. It was therefore proper to lend Dutch meeting-houses for English services when they were not required for their own.[6] In 1735 he reported that the English ministers in his neighborhood had increased to three, and that he was still accustomed to permit them to use the Dutch churches.[7] Here as everywhere the revival spirit tended to break down denominational exclusiveness. The main point of interest in this contention is that this group of Presbyterian ministers, so valiantly defended in their day of small things, was the nucleus of the New Brunswick presbytery, and that this presbytery became the head and front of the evangelistic movement in the Presbyterian denomination.

The splendid success and widening influence of Frelinghuysen had its background of vexatious opposition throughout his entire ministry and of serious bodily impairment through the greater part of it.[8] The development of the religious life of his adherents was made in a measure independent of his stated ministry by the introduction of two innovations in the several congregations. They demand a word of explanation.

The first of these, introduced by the domine very early, was private meetings for prayer very much after the pattern of the *collegia pietatis*

---

[1] *Eccl. Rec. of New York*, p. 2557.
[2] *Ibid.*, p. 2588.
[3] *Christian History* for 1744, p. 293.
[4] *Eccl. Rec. of New York*, pp. 2466, 2587.
[5] *Ibid.*, p. 2426.
[6] *Ibid.*, p. 2557.
[7] *Ibid.*, pp. 2667, 2678.
[8] *Ibid.*, pp. 2520, 2556, 2640; Frelinghuysen, *op. cit.*, pp. 211, 355.

of the German revival. The complainants in 1725 ask, "Is that the way to win souls, when one holds secret meetings, into which those whose souls are hungry are not admitted?"[1] In his memorial sermon of 1745 the domine announces that the prayer meetings "are hereafter to be held in public."[2] The inference is unavoidable that these private devotional meetings for twenty years or more were open only to converts and seekers whose loyalty to the new evangel could be trusted.

The justification for making these meetings private appears from their connection with another innovation of Frelinghuysen, the introduction of lay exhortation and lay preaching, a measure always opposed in the eighteenth century.[3] Apparently the first appointment of "helpers" was tentative and informal, but in 1736 there was the election by the united consistory of one or more lay helpers for each congregation.[4] They led these private devotional meetings and also the public meetings of the church in the absence of the pastor. In the public meetings their functions at first were no doubt those of the *voorleser*, but as several of them developed surprising powers of leadership and effective public address they insensibly passed from readers to exhorters and preachers. The most eminent of these helpers was Hendrick Fischer, whose sermons were published and were greatly prized in the valley as long as the language in which they were written remained in use.[5] In the evening of his life Fischer was the president of the New Jersey Provincial Congress and chairman of the Committee of Safety.[6] It was the church within the church which trained such laymen as Fischer and contributed to the high intellectual and spiritual character ultimately attained by the members of this group of churches.

Another measure by which Frelinghuysen extended his influence in New Jersey, New York, and in Holland itself was the frequent publication of sermons.[7] His writings made a stir, and no wonder, for they excelled in breadth of culture and emotional power.[8] These sermons were not only an instrumentality but a proof of the virility of the movement. The same may be said of the numerous church edifices which

---

[1] *Eccl. Rec. of New York*, p. 2275.   [2] Frelinghuysen, *op. cit.*, p. 360.

[3] Messler, *Memorial Sermons*, pp. 27, 171.

[4] *Ibid.*, p. 241; Steele, *Historical Discourse*, pp. 39, 41.

[5] Corwin's *Manual*, p. 271.   [6] Steele, *op. cit.*, p. 65.

[7] The last publication is not dated. These sermons were published in English in 1856.

[8] Messler, *Memorial Sermons*, p. 174; *Eccl. Rec. of New York*, p. 2698; Frelinghuysen, *op. cit.*, p. 10.

the energetic supporters of the revival erected, far outstripping in this practical demonstration of their faith their once more numerous and more wealthy opposers.

The genuineness of the man and the movement finally won the support of the moderate evangelicals who had feared what they considered the rashness of the leader. Chief among them was the genial Domine DuBois, senior pastor of the collegiate church of New York City. DuBois began to concert measures with those who desired greater independence for the establishment of a subordinate American classis.[1] This body was to be called a "coetus" and was to be subordinate to the classis of Amsterdam. No sooner did the progressive pastors, including those of evangelical sentiment, begin this movement than Domine Boel began a counter-movement showing irreconcilable opposition to the plan.

Such was the alignment of parties in the Dutch Reformed Church when Whitefield came in 1739 and again in 1740 as the apostle of the Great Awakening. Domine Boel denied him the use of the Dutch church,[2] but the senior pastor was ready to cast his great influence on the side of the revival.[3] How exasperating it was in 1740 to Domine Boel and his friend Commissary Vesey, of Trinity Church, to see the aged and popular DuBois uniting with Frelinghuysen and the Presbyterian minister, Pemberton, in the support of this reforming clergyman of the Church of England! These three ministers mounted the platform erected for the young orator, from which he preached to the assembled thousands.

Thus the story of the revival among the Dutch, as among the Germans, has been traced to the time when under the leadership of Whitefield the movement became general. Frelinghuysen had come to the Raritan Valley with the announced purpose of leading in a "purer reformation." He was rashly independent. His mission was to a people stubbornly conservative. He maintained a position concerning the qualifications for admission to church membership and communion table which was disavowed by the classis of Amsterdam,[4] a position which Gilbert Tennent and the New Side Presbyterians never distinctly attained,[5] and which was not advocated by Jonathan Edwards until after the close of the revival. When Jonathan Edwards changed his view upon the subject and abandoned his former practice and that of his

---

[1] *Eccl. Rec. of New York*, pp. 2679, 2681, 2694, 2715.

[2] *Ibid.*, p. 2798.   [3] *Ibid.*, p. 2799.   [4] *Ibid.*, p. 2678.

[5] Gilbert Tennent, *Irenicum*, p. 27.

eminent grandfather before him, he was dismissed from the pastorate of the Northampton church, much to his own humiliation, the surprise of all New England, and the everlasting regret of the church, which through its relation to him and the Great Awakening had become famous.[1]   Frelinghuysen, on the contrary, maintained his position at the head of four churches, not only from 1720 to 1739, but to the end of his life in 1748, and he was followed in the pastorate over those churches by men of his own blood and spirit.

[1] Dwight, *Edwards*, p. 305.

CHAPTER III

THE TENNENTS, AND THE BEGINNING OF THE REVIVAL AMONG THE PRESBYTERIANS

The work of William Tennent, of Log College fame, and of his sons and their associates was closely related to the work of Frelinghuysen, but the revival among the Presbyterians was more than an expansion of the revival among the Dutch Reformed. It was essentially an original movement, and therefore may be treated as the third distinct source of the Great Awakening in the Middle Colonies. To understand the course of the revival among the Presbyterians it is necessary to look at the historical background and see how like and yet unlike the Presbyterian Church in America was to its sister Reformed churches, the German and the Dutch.

When the presbytery of Philadelphia was formed in 1706 there was no organic connection with the churches in Scotland and Ireland. The new church in the colonies was not in a state of vassalage to the parent bodies. It was not necessary, therefore, to obtain permission in Europe to ordain candidates to the ministry. In other respects, especially in the matter of creed, the church did not reproduce the rigid lines of a national church. Had it done so it could never have possessed the propagating and assimilative power which made it the educator of a large section of the American people. The broad basis laid at the foundation of the church was due to the composite character of its membership, for while the major part was Scotch and Scotch-Irish, properly called Presbyterian, the minor part was New England Congregational, then also very generally called Presbyterian. The tremendous increase in the Presbyterian population in the Middle Colonies between the years 1706 and 1739 was due less to the absorption of New England Presbyterians than to the immigration from the north of Ireland.

A century of struggle had made the men of Ulster a race of iron and blood. Their coming to America rose almost to the proportions of a national exodus.[1] Those persecuted for religion were attracted to the colony where Penn had made the conscience free. They settled to some extent among the Quakers and Germans, but in great numbers they

[1] Thompson, *Presbyterians*, p. 23.

pushed, or were pushed, to the frontier. There they were exposed to Indian raids which were chargeable principally to French machinations but in part to their own aggressions.[1] The stream of immigration, deflected by the mountain walls and danger from the Indians, turned toward the southwest, following the Valley of Virginia. In this way the Presbyterians came into possession of the best lands of the southern provinces. Thus they occupied the frontier from New York to Georgia.

The Presbyterian immigrants who were clearing farms for themselves in the forests of Pennsylvania and other Middle Colonies entertained a static conception of Christianity.[2] The Westminster Confession was to them a finality. Precedent was invested with the authority of law. They were narrow, having no appreciation of the beauty of the English ritual and hating prelacy and the forms that brought to mind the tyranny under which they had suffered in Ireland. Their national prejudices were strong and yet they were chronically subject to divisions among themselves over infinitesimal questions of policy. These boisterous Ulstermen were not congenial neighbors to peace-loving Quakers and Mennonites,[3] and still less to the Indians, who were Canaanites in their eyes.[4]

It was natural, therefore, that among conservatives and formalists, such as the Irish Presbyterians were, men lacking the gentler graces of Christianity, the doctrine of the new birth was little known.[5] A deep conviction of sin, preparing the way for what the revivalists called "a saving closure with Christ," was stigmatized as "melancholy, trouble of the mind, or despair," whenever it did appear among this people. They were without that deep emotional experience which the Pietists denominated "the life of God in the soul of man." They were strangers to a consuming passion for God and personal righteousness. They made no pretension to a new heart with its new sympathy for the distressed and unfortunate of every race and creed. Therefore Rev. Samuel Blair says, not only of his own church at Fagg's Manor, Pennsylvania, which had been without a pastor from its erection in 1730 to the year 1739, but of the Scotch-Irish churches in general in those parts, that religion "lay dying and ready to expire its last breath."[6] The transplanting of this people from Scotland to Ireland involved a loss religiously

---

[1] Hanna, *The Scotch-Irish*, II, 64.

[2] Thompson, *op. cit.*, p. 24.   [3] Hanna, *op. cit.*, II, 63.

[4] Gordon, *The History of Pennsylvania*, p. 410; Thompson, *op. cit.*, p. 24.

[5] Samuel Blair in *Christian History* for 1744, p. 243.

[6] *Christian History* for 1744, p. 244.

and morally, and now a greater loss attended the removal to a wilderness.[1] There was no sufficient curb upon rampant appetites. This people was in danger of sinking to a condition of intellectual and moral degeneracy.

The leading men among the immigrants from Ireland appreciated the danger of barbarism, but as the people longed for religious advantages the hope seemed to be in a faithful ministry. Here a new danger confronted the infant church. The blight of Arianism had appeared in the church in Ireland, and ministers holding deistic and rationalistic principles were coming to the colonies. Others whose usefulness at home was destroyed by scandal sought in America to re-establish their reputations. There were instances in the colonies of seemingly good men falling victim to the prevailing laxity, and the church in its need of ministers too easily forgiving their offenses.[2] The majority of the Scotch-Irish ministers were men of high character, conservatives though they were, and they were alarmed at the danger to the church.

The problem was how to protect the Presbyterian Church from heretical and immoral ministers. A solution proposed at an early date by an influential section of the Scotch-Irish ministers, very natural to men trained in the rigid system of their native country, was enforced subscription to the Westminster Confession. Subscription had been used in Scotland to rid the church of prelatical ministers and in Ireland to drive out the Arians. In America the conservatives hoped to preserve orthodoxy by the same means.[3]

But to enforce subscription to a particular exposition of the Calvinistic system and to bring the local churches and their ministers under the strict surveillance of the central governing body would be a radical departure from the liberal policy adopted in 1706. The broad basis of union had brought a number of churches of New England origin into the Presbyterian Church. These churches and their pastors were not strict Presbyterians in their views upon church government. As a Puritan heritage they were more kindly disposed than were the Scotch-Irish, with a few significant exceptions, to the ideals of personal religion soon to be proclaimed by the evangelists of the Great Awakening. Jonathan Dickinson, of Elizabethtown, was the intellectual giant of the synod, for the one presbytery of 1706 was in 1722 a synod with four subordinate presbyteries. Among the American theologians of the period

---

[1] Thompson, *op. cit.*, p. 29.

[2] *Records of the Presbyterian Church*, pp. 61, 65, 137; Gillespie, *A Letter to the Presbytery of New York*, p. 27.

[3] Hodge, *Constitutional History of the Presbyterian Church*, Part I, p. 88; Thompson, *op. cit.*, p. 26.

he was second only to Jonathan Edwards.   According to Dickinson's sermon, preached before the synod of Philadelphia in 1722, Christ alone is the lawmaker of the church, and the church has only administrative functions.   It may decide upon rules in application of the general laws found in the New Testament, but these rules are not properly designated as acts or constitutions.[1]   They do not have the authority of laws.   A wide liberty should be left to the individual whose conscience does not permit him to follow them.[2]   Church judicatories may in cases of scandal and heresy try ministers for the violation of Christ's laws, but these courts ought not to censure ministers for the violation of ecclesiastical regulations against which their consciences rebel.   He concedes that a comprehensive creed may be useful, but insists that subscription to it must not be required.[3]   Such, in outline, was the masterful New England argument which stayed the hand of the conservative majority.

The Scotch-Irish conservatives were too much in earnest and too much alarmed by a real evil to cease the advocacy of their favorite measure.   Dickinson then published an answer to their latest overture. He advocated the strict examination of all candidates for the ministry before their admission to office.[4]   The result of this debate, which threatened to disrupt the infant church, was the adoption of a compromise in 1729.   All legislative power in the church was utterly disclaimed. Ministers were required to declare their agreement with the Westminster Confession "in all the essential and necessary articles," and if they entertained scruples with respect to any article they were to make declaration of these scruples, and the presbytery would decide whether the disagreement was upon essentials or not.   This was the famous Adopting Act.[5]

This line of division, which was drawn at first on the basis of nationality, Scotch-Irish against New Englander, came in course of time to be drawn between the conservative majority and the progressive and evangelical minority without reference to geographical origin.   Dickinson had advocated an examination not only of a candidate's belief but of his experience.   As the evangelical party grew, it more and more insisted upon the evidence of piety.   Gilbert Tennent, son of Ireland though he was, was a strenuous advocate of this principle.[6]   But the formalists held the view that any inquisitorial prying into the hidden

---

[1] Dickinson's *Sermon Preached at the Opening of the Synod*, p. 11.

[2] Hodge, *op. cit.*, Part I, p. 120.   [3] Dickinson, *op. cit.*, p. 22.

[4] Dickinson's *Remarks upon . . . . Overture*, p. 16.

[5] *Records of the Presbyterian Church*, p. 92.   [6] *Ibid.*, p. 108.

experiences of men was an assumption of the divine prerogative. They denied the right to judge candidates in this way but would pronounce men fit candidates if they possessed the necessary educational training, subscribed to the standards, and lived a moral life.[1] Thus in the years before the coming of Whitefield an evangelical and a conservative party formed in the Presbyterian Church. The one sought for essential orthodoxy; the other insisted on exact conformity to fixed standards. The one left the individual considerable latitude for self-direction when his conscience bade him protest against the administrative measures of the majority; the other held him to strict accountability to what it considered the laws of the church. The one emphasized piety as the first essential in a gospel ministry and sought for evidence of conversion and an inner call to the ministry; the other declared that it was a matter of conscience with conservatives not to institute such proceedings. A majority of New Englanders and a minority of the Scotch-Irish were members of the evangelical party. With few exceptions the leaders of both parties, New Sides and Old Sides, were sincerely devoted to truth as they saw it.

The course of the revival among the Presbyterians is unintelligible unless one grasps this distinction between the conservative and progressive parties. Furthermore, there was a distinction between the radical advocates of revivalism and the moderate evangelicals. While there were splendid figures among the New Englanders in the Middle Colonies, Dickinson, Pemberton, of New York, and Burr, of Newark, among them, warmly devoted to evangelical principles, they were not the chief promoters of the revival. They did not, above all others, prepare the way for Whitefield and continue his work. The itinerating evangelists that set the country on fire were, for the most part, Scotch-Irishmen. They were the ministers of the New Brunswick presbytery, the nucleus of which had been fostered by Domine Frelinghuysen, and members of other presbyteries who held close relations with this group. These evangelists were, with very few exceptions, graduates of the Log College, established by the elder Tennent at Neshaminy. This was the New Brunswick or radical New Side party.

William Tennent was a priest of the Church of Ireland who was graduated at the University of Glasgow, and whose wife was the daughter of a Presbyterian minister.[2] He became dissatisfied with the hierarchical system, as having no foundation in the Scriptures, and with the Arminian

---

[1] *Ibid.*, p. 319; Hodge, *op. cit.*, Part I, p. 204; Gillespie, *op. cit.*, p. 5.

[2] Briggs, *American Presbyterianism*, p. 186.

principles of the clergy.   Upon coming to America he was received into membership of the synod in September, 1718.[1]   He settled at East-chester, New York,[2] removing to Bensalem, Pennsylvania, in 1721.[3] Three years later he returned to New York.   He resided at Bedford and preached in the several towns of Westchester county with wondrous zeal.[4]   In 1726 he retraced his steps to the neighborhood of Bensalem and became pastor of the Presbyterian church at Neshaminy.[5]   He established an additional preaching station at Deep Run, twelve miles distant, and in 1732 this was erected into a church.   "William Tennent," according to Dr. C. A. Briggs, "was one of the greatest of the trophies won by Presbyterianism from Episcopacy in the first quarter of the eighteenth century."[6]   Webster, the conservative Presbyterian his-torian, concedes that "to William Tennent, above all others, is owing the prosperity and enlargement of the Presbyterian Church."[7]   No little interest therefore attaches to the sermon notes made by this father of Presbyterian education in America.   One time-stained paper con-tains the notes of a sacramental sermon preached in Ireland in 1717, when he was still a priest of the Irish church, and preached again at Bedford, New York, on December 1, 1724, when he was a minister of the Presbyterian Church.   In this sermon he distinguishes those who come to the Lord's Supper from those who really partake of it.   He insists on spiritual qualifications to the profitable partaking of the supper. Upon those not thus qualified exhortations are lost, and threatenings addressed to them are spoken to the wind.[8]   The elder Tennent was evidently an extemporaneous preacher, for his sermon notes required amplification in preaching—a sign in that day of the extreme evangelical. Though he is represented as having been a powerful preacher, and certainly he was very much of an itinerant, his great work was that of an educator.

William Tennent's study became a school for the education of his four sons.   Upon his settlement at Neshaminy in 1726, for the better accommodation of his school and the reception of other students, he built the log house which was called in derision the Log College.   The praises which Whitefield in his journal bestowed upon this school of the prophets

---

[1] *Records of the Presbyterian Church*, p. 49.   [2] Briggs, *op. cit.*, p. 187.

[3] Murphy, *The Presbytery of the Log College*, pp. 69, 197.

[4] Briggs, *op. cit.*, p. 187.   [5] Murphy, *op. cit.*, p. 70.

[6] Briggs, *op. cit.*, p. 187.

[7] Webster, *A History of the Presbyterian Church*, p. 367.

[8] MS in Presbyterian Historical Society Library at Philadelphia.

must have seemed extravagant to his readers, but the subsequent history of the sixteen or more graduates and the work which they performed as evangelists and educators justify the glowing words of the great orator.[1] It was the mother not only of Princeton but of many schools south and west and north. Other ministers prepared men for college or superintended their theological reading after their graduation, but the Log College gave ministerial candidates their college education and frequently their entire training. The scholarship which several of these men attained testifies to the thoroughness of their preparation under the instruction of Tennent, but what distinguished them above all others in the Presbyterian Church was their flaming evangelistic zeal. Piety had chief place in the curriculum.[2]

Where did the Log College get its sacred fire? Not from Domine Frelinghuysen, though his influence on Gilbert Tennent was great. The Pietism of Frelinghuysen but fanned the Puritanism of the Tennents. The religious teaching of the father was reflected in the religious experiences of the sons long years before they knew of the Dutch domine. When Gilbert Tennent was fourteen years old and his father was still a priest of the Church of Ireland, "he began to be seriously concerned for the salvation of his soul and continued so for several years, being often in great agony of spirit." After the usual preparatory studies he began the study of divinity, but his convictions that his state was bad did not permit him to entertain the purpose of entering the ministry. Therefore he began the study of medicine and continued it for a year, but the emotional experience which he regarded as essential came to him, and then, in the language of the time, "he was satisfied as to his interest in the divine favor."[3] Thus in his youth he held to the absolute necessity of conversion as a prerequisite to entrance into the ministry. Yet the Old Lights in New England and the Old Sides in the Middle Colonies stoutly contended that if a man were orthodox and moral he could be a useful minister even without conversion.

After the conversion of Gilbert Tennent and before he had permanently left the home of his parents his brother John experienced a far more cataclysmic change than his own had been. The life of the youth was "free from gross enormities," but "his conviction of sin," says Gilbert, "and the state of danger and misery he was brought into by it was the most violent in degree of any that ever I saw." It was in vain that the promises of Scripture were presented to the seeker.

[1] Whitefield, *Journal*, No. 5, p. 44.   [2] Alexander, *Log College*, pp. 20, 44.
[3] Finley, *The Successful Minister*, Appendix.

Finally, when John and his brother William were both so dangerously sick that their lives were despaired of, a rich discovery of God's love suddenly came to John, even when his death was momentarily expected. So rapidly did his strength return that in a few hours he was led exultantly to the room of his brother William.[1]   Both recovered.   Such experiences in the Tennent household were regarded, no doubt, by conservative Presbyterians as the excesses of enthusiasm, but the Tennents themselves never lost the deep impress of such crises in their family history.   Before Gilbert Tennent began to learn from Frelinghuysen the practical measures of the Pietists the Tennent household was thoroughly committed to the old Puritan conception of conversion.   The evangelistic fire of the Log College men must therefore be attributed primarily to William Tennent, their teacher.

The success of the sons of Tennent, presently to be related, brought a storm of criticism upon the Log College.   Conservatives feared that the Presbyterian Church would be deluged by a hoard of half-educated enthusiasts.   What then was the character of the instruction given at the Log College ?   Gilbert Tennent was the first English-speaking candidate for the ministry who received his education privately in the Middle Colonies, and not in the schools of New England or of the British Isles. The presbytery of Philadelphia approved highly of his qualifications.[2] After the usual trials he was licensed in May, 1725, and Yale College conferred on him the honorary degree of A.M. in the following autumn.[3] As required by the form of government, he was no doubt examined by the presbytery upon his knowledge of Hebrew, Greek, Latin, logic, philosophy, and divinity.[4]   It appears, therefore, that Gilbert Tennent, first graduate of the school afterward called the Log College, fairly met these requirements.

The published sermons of John Tennent, who died in 1732, throw light upon the character of the training in his father's school.   Each sermon has an elaborate exegetical introduction, abounding in Greek and Latin words, according to the taste of the time, while the body of the sermon contains quotations from the ancient fathers and from British theologians.   Gilbert Tennent says of his brother: "He made no contemptible progress in the learned languages and also in philosophical

[1] Alexander, op. cit., p. 100.

[2] Finley, op. cit., Appendix.

[3] Webster, ob. cit., p. 387.

[4] "Form of Church Government" in Confessions of Faith . . . . Church of Scotland, p. 180.

and theological studies; but he particularly excelled in the polemical and casuistical branches of divinity."[1]

Without attempting to present all the evidence upon the character of the instruction, the testimony concerning three other Log College men will be added. Samuel Blair studied five years at the Log College,[2] and we learn from his own pupil, Robert Smith, that frequently New Side preachers obtained their education in that time, though most of them studied longer.[3] Blair died in 1751, and Samuel Finley in his funeral sermon gave a very complete representation of the scholarly attainments of his friend and fellow educator. He speaks of Blair's store of critical learning, his scholarly habits in the impartial search for truth, and his independence of thought in reaching conclusions. He was especially conversant with the Scriptures in the original languages, and he made the knowledge of divinity the business of his life. His attainments in philosophy were known to few, but in his last years he had "greatly improved himself therein."[4] From this statement it is obvious that excellence in science, particularly the various branches of mathematics, then the vogue at Yale,[5] was not attributed to Log College men.

Such was President Finley's characterization of his friend, but of Finley himself it was said that he greatly surpassed his predecessor, President Davies, of Princeton, a student of Samuel Blair, "both in scholarship and skill in teaching," but that Davies had a more perfect acquaintance with English literature.[6] Again the inference is allowable that the training at the Log College emphasized the ancient classics to the neglect of modern literature.

When John Rowland died in 1745 Gilbert Tennent in his funeral sermon said of Rowland "that he was completely qualified for the ministerial work in respect of natural and acquired endowment, and excelled in those of a gracious nature."[7] Though the storm of conservative criticism broke upon the head of Rowland, there was no charge that his

---

[1] Alexander, *op. cit.*, p. 102.   [2] Murphy, *op. cit.*, p. 87.

[3] Robert Smith, *The Detection Detected*, p. 124.

[4] Alexander, *op. cit.*, p. 164.

[5] Thomas Clap, rector or president of Yale, 1739–66, was eminent as a mathematician. In 1758 Livingston, at the age of twelve, entered Yale. He was chiefly occupied during the first half of his collegiate life with the various branches of mathematics. In riper years he considered this time spent to little purpose. Gunn, *Memoirs of the Rev. John H. Livingston*, pp. 40–42.

[6] Alexander, *op. cit.*, p. 207.

[7] Gilbert Tennent, *A Funeral Sermon . . . . Rev. John Rowland*, p. 39.

preparation was in any respect different from that of other Log College men who had been regularly admitted into the ministry.

The answer to the question, therefore, is that William Tennent, graduate of Glasgow University, drilled his students thoroughly in the Latin and Greek languages.[1] He led them to an acquaintance with Hebrew. He taught them logic in such fashion that they became masterful debaters. He gave them a passion for theological study. The very atmosphere of the Log College was one of enthusiasm. But there were limitations in a school taught by one man who had received his own education many years before. Only for a little time did he have the assistance of his son Gilbert as usher. Therefore it may be assumed that the training was less efficient in the group of subjects embraced in the term "philosophy" than in the studies intimately connected with the practice of the ministerial profession.

Such was the training at the Log College. As a fitting school for ministers Whitefield pronounced it distinctly superior to the contemporary schools of New England and Europe.[2] When the four sons of Tennent—Gilbert, William, John, and Charles—and other early students, who were almost sons of the household by adoption, were successively admitted to the ministry, the older ministers, educated abroad or in New England, must have remarked the absence of that dignified carriage and polished manner which were then the badge of their order. Yet these young men were admirably trained, as has been described, and they felt themselves commissioned to propagate the warm type of religion which had been cultivated in their home. We are now to trace the actual beginning of the revival under their ministry.

When Gilbert Tennent began his work at New Brunswick in 1726 Domine Frelinghuysen was doubtful of the expediency of his own people encouraging this English preaching, since Joseph Morgan, an opposer of evangelistic methods, was one of the ministers who laid hands upon the young candidate. The effort of the new preacher at first was to build up a congregation and to commend his church and his person to the favor of the English-speaking people. His success in this was such that both the pious and the profane delighted in his sermons and in his intercourse with them.[3]

Then he was taken ill and lamented the barrenness of his ministry, comparing it with the success of the domine. He received a letter

---

[1] Alexander, *op. cit.*, p. 20.

[2] Whitefield, *Journal*, for November 22, 1739.

[3] Finley, *op. cit.*, Appendix.

from Frelinghuysen that excited him to greater earnestness and to the adoption of the domine's method of preaching.[1] When he resumed his work, therefore, he directed his message so pointedly to each class among his hearers that every person imagined that he heard his own case described. No longer did the speaker restrain his emotions; he gave uncurbed expression to them. Indeed, like Frelinghuysen, upon occasion he could pour the vials of vituperation upon the heads of opposers. He passed beyond the domine in his vivid portrayal of threatened doom. Some left his preaching with disgust. They charged him with blasphemy, "as assuming the divine prerogative of being a searcher of hearts, and pretending to know, by seeing a man's face, whether he would be saved or damned."[2] The Dutch complainants reported to classis that even the English leader who had approached them for their subscriptions had himself become displeased and now had nothing more to do with Tennent.[3] A greater number of his hearers were sobered by the new earnestness of their preacher, and many, though few at a time, experienced the change by which religion became the dominant force in their lives. Indeed there were seasons when feeling was so general and strong that some "were compelled to cry out in the public assembly, both under the impression of terror and love."[4] This phenomenon occurred at New Brunswick and other preaching stations, but it was most marked on Staten Island about the year 1729.

It was a little more than three years after Gilbert Tennent began to gather the varied elements of his congregation that John Tennent came to a long-established Scotch congregation. John was licensed in the autumn of 1729 and with the leave of the presbytery of Philadelphia preached a few Sabbaths at Freehold, New Jersey. He found the congregation in such a distracted condition that it was thought that there could never be agreement upon the settlement of another pastor.[5] Yet the young licentiate told the members that "if they called him he would settle among them, albeit he should be put to beg his bread by so doing."[6] His frankness and engaging manners won him a unanimous

---

[1] *Christian History* for 1744, p. 293.

[2] Finley, *op. cit.*, Appendix.

[3] *Ecclesiastical Records of the State of New York*, p. 2589.

[4] *Christian History* for 1744, p. 295.

[5] Joseph Morgan had been pastor of this church, though giving the greater part of his time to Dutch churches. He was an opposer of Frelinghuysen. He was now pastor at Maidenhead.

[6] *Christian History* for 1744, p. 300.

call, though his people well understood his adherence to the evangelical doctrines which Morgan, his predecessor, had ridiculed.[1]

The preaching of John Tennent was vibrant with emotion, but while his brother Gilbert overwhelmed his hearers with the threat of doom, John's voice was mellowed by a sense of the divine pity. People of every sort flocked to hear him. While the great majority did not accept his teaching upon the necessity of regeneration, at least of regeneration as he defined it, religious discussion became general. Bible study was widely practiced, and there was a perceptible alteration in the moral conduct of the people. He wept over his sermons in their preparation, and frequently their delivery moved the whole congregation to tears. It was no uncommon thing to see persons sobbing as if their hearts would break, and there were instances of people being carried out quite overcome. Yet there was no crying out, as had been the case under the preaching of Gilbert Tennent.[2]

The affectionate regard of the people for their young minister waxed the warmer as they saw him failing in health. His brother William, who was older than John, but did not so soon finish his studies, came to preach in his stead for the last six months of his life. The old father came to deliver what was almost a funeral sermon a little more than a month before the young man died. The text of that sermon compares human life with the grass which flourishes in the morning but in the evening is cut down and withers.[3] John Tennent died in April, 1732. Before that date there were many conversions, but for some months after his death the number was much larger than at any time during his life.[4]

William Tennent, Jr., was admirably fitted to continue the work of his brother, for he too was a mystic.[5] The spell of his recent trance was upon him. He was not aggressive and combative, like Gilbert, but retiring. He would have preferred to weep and pray in some lodge in the wilderness rather than to contend with opposition. Yet his influence was powerful and wholesome. The reformation at Freehold was

---

[1] *Records of the Presbyterian Church*, p. 135.

[2] *Christian History* for 1744, p. 300.

[3] MS sermon of W. Tennent, Sr., March 13, 1731, in Presbyterian Historical Society Library.

[4] *Christian History* for 1744, p. 301.

[5] Not that he was a member of a mystical order or adherent of a mystical philosophy, but that the mystical element, strong in all Pietists and revivalists, was especially pronounced in him.

permanent. William Tennent lived to become the Nestor of his denomination. The church in which he preached and which to-day is affectionately called "Old Tennents" has become the Presbyterian pilgrim shrine of New Jersey.

Gradually there settled on every side of New Brunswick ministers who, like Gilbert Tennent, were actively devoted to evangelism. John Cross, a Scotchman, was at Basking Ridge, in the upland country north of the Raritan Valley, called "the mountain back of Newark." He led a remarkable revival in 1734 and 1735. Three hundred conversions were reported.[1] His influence was great in that extensive region, and he was much in demand as an itinerant evangelist. Unfortunately he held antinomian principles, valuing religious emotion for its own sake, apart from its connection with moral renovation.[2] In 1734 Samuel Blair, one of the brightest lights of the Log College, settled at Shrewsbury and served a number of scattered congregations. Eleazer Wales, a Yale graduate, came to New Jersey about 1730 and settled at Kingston, on the Millstone, a tributary of the Raritan, in 1735. He was a faithful supporter of the evangelical movement. Thus the three Log College men with Cross and Wales constituted a radical party, while the pastors of churches of New England origin in the older section of New Jersey, led by Dickinson, though evangelical in sentiment, were not yet drawn into this active movement. The natural line of cleavage was followed when in 1738 the presbytery of New Brunswick was erected with these five ministers as members.[3]

Thus in 1738 the ministers who were actually engaged in the propagation of a revival, and who, themselves thoroughly aroused, were trying to awaken their brethren, were few. They were mostly confined to the little group which was led by Gilbert Tennent and was erected by the synod into the presbytery of New Brunswick. These zealous revivalists possessed in the Log College, though Neshaminy was within the bounds of the presbytery of Philadelphia, not only a school where young candidates were given a splendid intellectual training, but a school where

---

[1] This incident is remarkable, not for the number of conversions, but that any number at all is given. It was not the custom of Whitefield or of the various pastors who published detailed reports of the course of the revival in their congregations to state the number of conversions. Any estimate, therefore, of the number of conversions in the Great Awakening is a mere guess, which I refrain from making. Whitefield, *Journal*, No. 5, p. 41.

[2] This led to his undoing and suspension by the presbytery in 1742. Webster, *op. cit.*, p. 414.

[3] *Records of the Presbyterian Church*, p. 136.

their enthusiasm for the revival was fanned to white heat. And now they had been regularly constituted a presbytery, the immemorial privilege of which, according to the Directory, was the licensing and ordaining of candidates suitably prepared.[1] It was for this that they desired to be made a presbytery.[2]

The privilege of examining and ordaining young men prepared at the Log College, which was given by the institution of the presbytery of New Brunswick, was in effect withdrawn at the same meeting of the synod by the adoption of an overture proposed by the presbytery of Lewes.[3] This was a small body of small men. The lack of university opportunities and of skilled professors within the bounds of the synod was held forth at great length, with never a word of appreciation of the singularly gifted teacher, William Tennent, who was at that moment training a band of promising young men at the Log College. The implication was that the men already admitted to the ministry from that school were insufficiently qualified. Yet there was not a minister among the conservatives, except Francis Alison, whose scholarly attainments equaled those of Samuel Blair. There was not another man in the synod who developed the pulpit power of Gilbert Tennent or who could show the success in the ministry of William Tennent, Jr.

By the new regulation presbyteries were permitted to examine and ordain candidates who produced the diplomas of New England or European colleges. But candidates without such diplomas were to be previously examined by a committee of the synod, and the certificates of such committee were to be presented to the presbytery in lieu of diplomas. The unfriendliness of the measure to the Log College was further shown in the personnel of the two examining committees. College professors had a voice in the granting of diplomas to their students, but William Tennent was not recognized so far as to be appointed on either of the committees.[4]

The animus of this legislation is made the clearer by other acts of this same year and the year before, framed to hold in check the young evangelists prepared at the Log College. It was enacted that no probationer should supply any vacancy without the permission both of the presbytery to which he belonged and of the presbytery to which the congregation belonged.[5] Neither was an ordained minister, although

[1] *Confessions of Faith*, p. 179.

[2] Whitefield, *Journal*, No. 5, p. 44.

[3] *Records of the Presbyterian Church*, p. 139.

[4] *Ibid.*, p. 140.   [5] *Ibid.*, p. 133.

a member of the synod, permitted to supply any congregation not belonging to his presbytery, if a single minister of the presbytery to which the congregation belonged protested. It mattered not whether he came upon the invitation of a vacant congregation or of a settled pastor; it was in the power of a single opposer of the revival to forbid such service until the presbytery or synod gave its permission.[1] It was hostility to the Log College and to the militant evangelism cultivated there that caused the enactment of these laws. No wonder that Gilbert Tennent cried out in one of the meetings that the synod aimed "to prevent his father's school from training gracious men for the ministry."[2]

It is a surprise, therefore, upon turning the yellow pages of the treasured minutes of the New Brunswick presbytery to find how evident was the purpose that every action, taken only after prayerful deliberation, should conform to order and precedent. Frequent meetings were held in widely separated places. Though each pastor was more or less of an itinerant locally, he was assigned in addition long preaching tours to destitute congregations and new settlements—all within the bounds of the presbytery. These men were too busy to intrude upon other pastors, but at their first meeting they licensed John Rowland, who had finished his course of study at the Log College, and in due time they ordained him, just as they did many others in the succeeding years, all in defiance of the law of the synod forbidding such licensure and ordination.[3] They fell back upon the arguments of Jonathan Dickinson, leader of the New Englanders in the synod, presented in 1722 and 1729. Christ is the lawmaker; the New Testament is the law. Presbyterian directories and accredited writers have all along defended this right of presbyteries to examine and ordain candidates by appeal to the Scriptures. When the synod attempts to deprive a presbytery of this right it exercises a legislative power which it disclaimed in 1729, and which the presbytery of New Brunswick refuses to concede to it. Indeed this power, they think, opens the door to intolerable bondage. The other act of 1738 was, in their view, uncharitable and gave a commission to every membe of a presbytery to play the tyrant.[4]

Not only did they license and ultimately ordain John Rowland, a man of extraordinary power, but they recommended his acceptance

[1] *Ibid.*, p. 136. [2] *Ibid.*, p. 185.

[3] Yet there was unusual deliberation with adjournments. MS Minutes of the New Brunswick Presbytery for August 8, 1738; September 5, 1739; and October 11, 1739.

[4] Hodge, *op. cit.*, Part II, pp. 104–8; *Records of the Presbyterian Church*, p. 144.

of the invitation of the New Side churches of Maidenhead and Hopewell. These towns were just outside the bounds of the New Brunswick presbytery. The former pastor, Morgan, an opposer of the revival, had been suspended by the synod for drunkenness. There was a separation of evangelicals and conservatives. The former were erected by the presbytery of Philadelphia into separate congregations with liberty "to invite any regular candidate from other parts to preach among them." If the regulation of the synod requiring previous examination by its committee was beyond the competency of the synod there was no irregularity in Rowland's acceptance of the invitation of these neighboring churches, but if the first-named action of the synod was constitutional Rowland was guilty of intrusion.[1]

To observe the course of the revival at Maidenhead, Hopewell, and Amwell[2] apart from the contest over Rowland's entrance into the ministry it is necessary to return to the time of his licensure. A rural community sharply divided into two factions, each served by a young licentiate, was not the probable scene of a helpful quickening of the religious life. Yet there was an awakening in these three townships quite as remarkable as the earlier reformations at New Brunswick, Freehold, and Basking Ridge. Mr. Gould, the minister-elect of the conservatives, was a quiet, conciliatory man, under whom the New Sides and Old Sides ultimately united. It was a pity that the Presbyterians of the three towns did not unite under the two men whose gifts were complementary, but in 1738 the division of sentiment among the people did not permit of this, and the alleged irregularity of Rowland's license was a barrier. At first Rowland was denied the use of the meeting-houses at Maidenhead and Hopewell, and, like Frelinghuysen before him, he preached in barns. So great were the congregations that the largest barns of his adherents were required. Later he was granted the use of the meeting-house at Maidenhead, and a new one was built in the township of Hopewell. At Amwell he did not meet with organized opposition, but, though he found the people agreeable, few in the beginning were deeply interested in religion.[3]

The debate among the people was quickly turned from the knotty problems of ecclesiastical law and the unfortunate division in the com-

---

[1] Hale, *A History of the Old Presbyterian Congregations of . . . . Maidenhead and Hopewell*, pp. 56, 110–12; Gilbert Tennent, sermons on "The Solemn Scene" and on "Duty" published with *Unsearchable Riches*.

[2] Amwell was within the bounds of the presbytery of New Brunswick.

[3] Rowland, *A Narrative of the Revival*.

munity to the deeper question of personal relation to God. For six long months Rowland with terrible earnestness preached upon the two themes, conviction and conversion. The most arousing texts were selected. Though he divided his ministry among three townships, the interest was not permitted to subside by long intervals between meetings in one neighborhood. Sunday-night meetings were introduced, a marked innovation in the eighteenth century, and week-day meetings, so that the young enthusiast was constantly going from one service to another. Presently the one topic of conversation in these towns was heart religion. Everyone was asking himself whether he was really converted. A deep gloom began to settle over the three New Side congregations. Now one person and now another broke down and owned himself convicted. Yet the months passed, and the prophet of woe but increased their anguish by his arraignment of sin and declaration of the divine displeasure.[1]

Finally, when the number of the convicted was very considerable, and the people who looked upon themselves as converted were aroused to earnest effort in their behalf, the preacher changed his method. The most inviting and encouraging subjects were taken. The eye that had flashed with the anger of God was now a well of tears. Solemn weeping came over the congregation. From this time on conversions were more numerous. Sometimes it was the aged to whom the joy of pardon came, and sometimes it was the children. The negroes were included in the invitation, and Rowland reports that some were very earnest after the word. Kindly Christian fellowship found new ways of expression in the three congregations. The little differences which often trouble good people were practically unknown among them.[2]

The movement spread beyond the circle of families which originally composed the three New Side congregations. While Rowland does not report the conversion of any who at first opposed the revival, many who had been quite indifferent to the claims of religion were reached. Again there were some who were little affected by the doctrine of the new birth when it was first preached among them, but who three years later were visibly affected. There were striking illustrations of the power of Rowland's preaching. At one meeting in 1739, just before the arrival of Whitefield, only fifteen persons were present, owing to an insufficient "warning," as the circulation of an invitation in a neighborhood was called. Not being dependent upon the number of his listeners, he was carried quite out of himself by the awful purport of his message, when

[1] *Ibid.*   [2] *Ibid.*

suddenly he was compelled to stop by the outcries of his hearers.   Surprised, he asked why they cried out in such a manner.   The answer of some was "that they saw hell opening before them, and themselves ready to fall into it."   The most remarkable outbursts of feeling were in spontaneous gatherings in private houses.   Some of the largest accessions were in 1740, when the movement, so far as conversions were concerned, had apparently spent itself for lack of new material.   Rowland reports that sometimes when he cast the gospel net many slipped out as soon as they were caught.   Yet of the multitude that gave evidence of conversion no considerable number were reckoned as backsliders in after-times when the period of stress had given place to the ordinary routine of life and feeling.[1]

From the foregoing account two characteristics of the Presbyterian revival in New Jersey must have been noted by the reader.   The first is that the conservative majority in control of the church, centering at Philadelphia but strongest on the frontier of Pennsylvania, aimed to restrict the troublesome promoters of strenuous religion to a sharply defined territory in New Jersey and to cripple their power of action even within that territory.   The second characteristic is that the revival fire did not leap from town to town and rapidly envelop a wide stretch of country in a general conflagration, as in the New England revival of 1734.   The Edwards revival of 1734 spread throughout western Massachusetts and the adjoining colony of Connecticut, and in its special phenomena came to an end.   It was so like the larger movement of 1740 that it is often represented as the beginning of the Great Awakening. The revivals in New Brunswick and Freehold were earlier than the beginning of the Edwards revival at Northampton, but the fire was not immediately carried to neighboring settlements.   The diversities among the people in blood and sentiment and their less compact organization were obstacles to a movement like that in western Massachusetts.   Nevertheless the several revivals which have been traced in this chapter were parts of a whole, for the promoters of them acted in close co-operation, and the reports of startling events in one town stimulated the desire of the pious in other towns for a like spiritual rejuvenation.

It was the common appreciation of the power of publicity that suggests another comparison of the Freehold awakening of 1732 with the Northampton awakening of 1734.   The Edwards revival had widespread influence in America and abroad through the printed reports which were given to the public, but Gilbert Tennent was also prompt in summoning

[1] Rowland, *A Narrative of the Revival.*

the printing-press to his aid. In 1734 he sent to the press the two sermons of his brother John on regeneration and adoption, with a biographical sketch of their author. In 1735 he published at Boston a "Solemn Warning," based on fear, and strongly justified his method in an introduction. This discourse was terrifying in its denunciation of sin and threat of judgment. He also published that year "An Expostulatory Address," which was based upon the complementary idea of the winning power of divine love. Here he applied the method of persuasion so successfully employed at Freehold. In this discourse, with abandonment of restraint, he revealed that warmth of sympathy which so endeared him to his friends. This address and the sermons of John Tennent were published in London in 1741 under the patronage of Whitefield. Thus the printed accounts of the revival in New Jersey contributed in the colonies to an expectation of an outburst of the old-time Puritan fervor, and in England later the rough but vigorous words of these Log College men added force to a movement already begun. This expectation was heightened when the report of the work in the Highlands and in the three towns of Maidenhead, Hopewell, and Amwell, so potent and mysterious, was carried to every quarter. Above all, the almost incredible stories of the success of George Whitefield in the home land gave promise of a general revival. It was a time gladdened by hope, and yet hope tempered by dread.

CHAPTER IV

GEORGE WHITEFIELD, AND HIS ALLIANCE WITH THE NEW BRUNSWICK PRESBYTERIANS

Three contributory streams have been traced to their point of junction. They have been broadly designated as the German, Dutch, and Scotch-Irish contributions to the Great Awakening. The breadth and power of these movements are not to be measured by the number and duration of such local revivals as have been described. An increasing number of people were beginning to shake off the lethargy of their times; they longed for a religion of energy and passion. Hoping, despairing, praying, struggling, they measurably attained it. These were the evangelicals. Some of the pastors were thrilled by the vision of a new reformation; their very faces reflected the inner light. Here and there this growing interest became intense and passionate, attended by numerous conversions which were often so revolutionary and extraordinary that the strange visitation seemed miraculous. The story of each community thus visited was carried by the winds to every quarter, stimulating the religious desires of thousands, spurring evangelical pastors to greater earnestness and warmth, and binding them together in close fraternity. In spite of the frowns of the coldly intellectual, still constituting a majority of the church members, the country was ready to be swept by a wave of emotionalism, if only a leader could be found who was broad in sympathy, deep in emotional experience, and commissioned by a prophet's gift of utterance. This leader was found in George Whitefield.

But just as these three streams were to unite in a seething flood of emotionalism, a fourth source of the Great Awakening in the Middle Colonies added its contribution. If this were a study of the whole intercolonial movement, unquestionably the New England revival of 1734 would be considered as the most important, though not the earliest, of the several contributory movements. But the Edwards revival had no direct and immediate effect upon the Middle Colonies. The Presbyterian congregations of New England origin, located mostly on Long Island and in East Jersey, whether incorporated with the synod or still independent, were for the most part evangelical in sentiment, though their pastors were not in full harmony with the more radical Log College men. Some of these pastors had been converted in the Edwards revival, and now, years after that revival had come to an end, a very similar religious interest began to appear in their congregations. The most important of these local revivals was at Newark under the pastorate of the brilliant Aaron Burr.[1] It began in August, 1739, and gathered momentum from month to month. Other pastors in the neighborhood were hoping for its spread to their congregations.[2] While these transplanted New England towns were, no doubt, stirred by the reports of the renewed power of religion among the various nationalities west of them, the strongest incentive was their intimate acquaintance with the New England awakening of 1734. The Edwards revival was thus itself revived, and just before the landing of Whitefield became one of the sources of the Great Awakening in this section of the country.

While these four religious movements, more or less independent of each other, were essentially parts of one general and even world movement, this was not patent to all until Whitefield came as the chief apostle of the Great Awakening. Not till then were men everywhere arrested by the call of the Spirit. Not till then did every other issue pale in the general debate upon religion. Furthermore, not till his coming was a sustained interest manifested by the people of one colony in the course of events, whether religious or secular, in the sister colonies,[3] but all ears were open for news from "home." The newspapers were filled with transcripts from the London papers. At this point it will be appropriate to give an ampler representation than that in the opening chapter of the preparation for the Great Awakening made by the newspapers through the publication of startling accounts of Whitefield's career before he landed at Lewes, Delaware, on October 30, 1739. These accounts also give us a fresh view of the man who was soon to electrify greater audiences than had ever before gathered within the hearing of a single voice in the colonies.

With this twofold purpose we turn over the time-stained pages of the colonial papers. The *Virginia Gazette* tells of the great concourse of people that filled the church of St. Mary Magdalene, London, long before the time of service, and of several hundred persons in the street who in vain endeavored to force themselves into the church and past the constables stationed at the door to preserve the peace. Such was the

---

[1] *Christian History* for 1743, p. 252; Stearns, *Historical Discourse*, p. 156.

[2] *Christian History* for 1743, p. 254.

[3] Hoskins, "German Influence," *Princeton Theological Review* (1907), pp. 70–73.

mad desire to see and hear the eloquent youth who had volunteered to go to Georgia as a missionary.[1]   Directly a longer article appeared in the *Mercury*, published at Philadelphia, stating the amounts of collections for charity schools taken at these services.[2]   But a discordant note was sounded when an English paper, the *Weekly Miscellany*, began an anti-Methodistic campaign by the publication of articles against enthusiasm. Next there was the announcement in the *South Carolina Gazette* of White-field's departure from London on his way to Georgia.[3]   The last-named paper and all the others to the northward were strangely silent on his movements in Georgia, his resolution to found an orphan house, even his preaching in Charleston and his return to England to receive priest's orders.   But when he was once again in England the papers from end to end of the colonies were filled with reports of his phenomenal career.

It was these later reports especially that excited curiosity to hear him and fanned the hopes of the pious when it was learned that he was about to visit the Middle Colonies.   He was ordained at Oxford on January 14, 1739,[4] and sailed for America on August 14, following.   In the interval he journeyed about England in the interest of his projected orphan house, but it very soon developed that his peculiar calling was that of an evangelist.   The papers had told of riots among the colliers at Bristol consequent upon a reduction of their wages from sixteen pence to a shilling.[5]   Some months after these riots Whitefield visited Bristol and, being refused the churches, preached in the open to these abused, besotted colliers.[6]   Thus began his famous field preaching. Sometimes the accounts of his movements were taken from the London papers, and sometimes they appeared to be summary reports sent directly to America.   Highly laudatory verses were copied from the *Gentleman's Magazine*.[7]   When Whitefield had returned to London from this tour the papers told of his preaching from a tombstone, for the warden of a church in which he had been invited by the vicar to preach denied him the pulpit.[8]   Then the colonial readers were informed of his preaching

[1] *Virginia Gazette*, January 6, 1738.

[2] *American Weekly Mercury*, January 24, 1738.

[3] *South Carolina Gazette*, May 4, 1738.

[4] Whitefield, *Journal*, No. 3, p. 9.

[5] New York *Gazette*, February 27, 1739.

[6] *Ibid.*, May 7, 1739.

[7] *American Weekly Mercury*, June 21, 1739.

[8] Boston *Gazette*, June 25, 1739.

to twenty thousand people and even to fifty thousand on Kensington Common and at Moorfields.[1]

According to some of the accounts his preaching had become an offense to the clergy of the Church of England,[2] but a dissenter wrote to his ministerial friend in the colonies of these Methodists as providentially raised up to lead a reformation from profaneness to piety.[3] Indeed already the face of things had been changed in parts of Wales through the efforts of men of a spirit kindred to Whitefield's. The simple but fundamental doctrines into which he breathed the spirit of life the descendants of the Puritans read in their century-old books. His fidelity to the articles of his church, which were Calvinistic in character, and the closing of pulpits against him by his brethren commended the evangelist not a little to pious dissenters in the colonies.

When Whitefield landed in Delaware in 1739 on his way to Georgia he came with certain prepossessions which greatly affected his ministry. The first of these was a spirit of censoriousness, a disposition to judge his critics rashly. This was due to the peculiar experiences of his brief career and was foreign to his generous nature. Therefore a larger experience in the world corrected this tendency in a very few years,[4] but the wild-fire by that time had spread, so that from his day to the present censoriousness has been the fault in a class of itinerant evangelists whose influence in other respects has been good.[5]

A glance at these experiences easily accounts for this unfortunate habit. As a member of the Holy Club at Oxford he came to look upon himself and his Methodist associates as a band of faithful disciples

[1] *South Carolina Gazette*, September 1, 1739. When Whitefield was preaching to a great throng in Philadelphia from the court-house steps Franklin walked down the street "till the speaker's voice was obscured by the noise of the street." Then imagining a semicircle, filled with auditors, to each one of whom he allowed two square feet, he computed that more than thirty thousand could hear the preacher, so loud and clear was his voice and so perfectly articulated were his words. This reconciled Franklin to the newspaper accounts of Whitefield's preaching in England. Franklin, *Autobiography*, pp. 132, 133.

[2] New York *Gazette*, November 19, 1739.

[3] Boston *News-Letter*, November 15, 1739.

[4] Whitefield, *Some Remarks on a Pamphlet entitled, The Enthusiasm of Methodists and Papists compar'd*, pp. 14, 16.

[5] The writer in his own ministry has had experience with evangelists of this type and in his studies has found them appearing in every period. As Whitefield was the greatest evangelist of the eighteenth century his faults as well as his virtues were imitated.

persecuted and held in scorn by a multitude of nominal Christians.[1]
Ministers called him an enthusiast.   His first journals, which he had
sent home from Georgia, were, contrary to his directions, published without editing.[2]   Therefore the private thoughts of an ardent youth concerning his elders in the ministry, mentioning them by name, were
published to the world.   His journals were immensely popular and went
through many editions.   Though he was more circumspect in later
numbers, it was impossible not to offend.   Then returning to England
he was greeted by a fierce storm of opposition.   Mobs were set upon him.
Yet the people hung on his words, and strong hearts were melted by his
ministry.   He came into friendly relations with Griffith Jones and Howell
Harris, who had brought reformation to Wales in spite of years of liti-
gation and persecution by the clergy.[3]   Whitefield concluded that the
possessors of genuine piety in his own church were but a remnant.[4]

He had but little reason to think better of non-conformists.   Though
he was taunted with being a dissenter,[5] most dissenters in his country
held aloof from him, unable to overcome their prejudices and fearful
of the effects of his untempered zeal.   He was a correspondent of the
Erskines in Scotland.   Their expulsion by a corrupt majority in temporary control of the general assembly but confirmed his opinion, common
with the aggressive promoters of vital religion, that the body of the
ministry in all lands was unconverted.[6]   The battles forced upon the
pacific Spener in Germany and upon his successor, Francke, were additional evidences.   Therefore he came to the colonies prepared to accept
the opinion of Frelinghuysen and the Tennents concerning the majority of ministers of all denominations in the American possessions.

Thus Whitefield was predisposed to give hearty support only to men
who like himself advocated a religion of energy and passion; furthermore he liked such men the better if they were Calvinists in their religious
philosophy, for when he landed at Lewes he was already a Calvinist.
Before his ordination as deacon he thoroughly compared the Thirty-nine
Articles with Scripture, verifying them, in his opinion, and therefore in
subscribing to them he gave unqualified assent to their truth.[7]   Though
his study at first was almost entirely in pietistic literature, his interest

---

[1] Whitefield, *Brief Account*, p. 26.

[2] Whitefield, *Journal*, No. 2, Preface.

[3] Tyerman, *Wesley*, I, 221.

[4] Whitefield, *Journal*, No. 3, pp. 75, 109.   [5] *Ibid.*, p. 39.

[6] *Ibid.*, p. 97; Gledstone, *George Whitefield*, p. 97.

[7] Whitefield, *Brief Account*, p. 56.

being in regeneration and conversion, ʌ
drawn on to "the whole counsel of ᴜ
intimacy with Howell Harris stimulated t
voyage across the Atlantic in 1739 he gave
istic attacks upon Arminianism.[2] These sᴜ
rupture with churchmen in America and to ᴠ
numerous dissenters. An itinerant missionaᴧ
Whitefield in Christ Church, Philadelphia, durinᵷ
him with making man a machine.[3] Neverthelᴇ   ̣y
expressions in his journals and printed sermons w   ̣en to
criticism by strict Calvinists.[4] He had been deeᵖ   ̣uenced by
German mystics and Moravians, though escaping some ᴜᵣ their practices
which were freely adopted by John Wesley.

In spite of his gradually stiffening Calvinism a marked characteristic
of Whitefield was his catholic spirit. It is true that in general evangelicals as compared with conservatives had little denominational prejudice,
but Whitefield was extraordinary in his sympathetic attitude toward
Christians of all names who were promoters of vital religion. On his
voyage to America in 1739 he even lent his cabin to a Quaker preacher,
who held meetings there. Whitefield consented freely to the Friend's
teaching upon the Christ within but regretted his slight of the objective
Christ and the ordinances instituted by him.[5] Then too Whitefield
had spent pleasant hours of Christian conference with Baptists, though he
himself held the Episcopal theory of ordination and of the real presence
of Christ in the elements of the Lord's Supper.[6] In England he had
collected money for the Lutherans of Georgia[7] and enjoyed fellowship
with the Moravians, though his Calvinism was a barrier to the fullest
intercourse with them.[8]

With these predispositions Whitefield arrived at Lewes. We are
now to follow the gradual alignment of forces and the marshaling of the
cohorts of militant righteousness. But though Whitefield believed himself the possessor of a prophet's call and knew full well the power of his
oratory, he was, withal, a gentleman and entertained no purpose of
antagonizing those who were not in full agreement with him. He

---

[1] Gledstone, *op. cit.*, p. 116.   [2] Whitefield, *Journal*, No. 5, p. 19.

[3] New York *Post-Boy*, January 21, 1745.

[4] Whitefield, *A Letter . . . . in Answer to . . . . Querists*, p. 61; Franklin,
op. cit., p. 134.

[5] Whitefield, *Journal*, No. 5, p. 16.   [7] *Ibid.*, No. 3, p. 7.

[6] *Ibid.*, No. 4, pp. 7, 12, 24.   [8] *Ibid.*, No. 3, p. 97.

ewes, the adherents of various denominations attending, gh the minister "subscribed to the articles of the Church of and in his own sense" he opened his pulpit to Whitefield then, and again the following year.[1] This was more considerate treatment than he had learned to expect in England. The same privilege was accorded him at Philadelphia by Commissary Cummings. The newspapers record that he preached in Christ Church every day, "people of all persuasions going to hear him."[2] A week later, besides the morning service in the church, he added an afternoon service in the open air. This he excuses as a concession to the sentiment of the province. Thereupon the papers say that he had begun "to preach from the court-house gallery at six at night to near six thousand people before him in the street, who stood in awful silence to hear him." He did not make public appeals for gifts toward the building of his orphan house during the time of this journey, though goods given in England for this purpose were offered for sale in Philadelphia.[3] Delighted with the warmth of his welcome he announced through the papers his future plans, first that he intended to visit all the southern provinces on his way to Georgia,[4] and later that he would preach the gospel in every province before his return to England.[5]

During his visit at Philadelphia he had intercourse with members of the Society of Friends, exceeding kindness being shown him by some of them. He speaks of them as honest, open-hearted, and true.[6] The Presbyterian and Baptist ministers came to his lodgings to tell of their pleasure in hearing "Christ preached in the Church." There is no intimation yet that the former, Jedediah Andrews and Robert Cross, would become bitter opposers, and the latter, Jenkin Jones, his special

[1] Whitefield, *Journal*, No. 5, p. 25; No. 6, p. 49; *Pennsylvania Gazette*, November 8, 1739.

[2] *American Weekly Mercury*, November 8, 1739. Franklin says, "The multitudes of all sects and denominations that attended his sermons were enormous." He adds that when Whitefield preached from the court-house steps in the middle of Market Street, both Market and Second streets were filled with his hearers to a considerable distance. Franklin gives no hint that the reports in his own and other papers of the number of Whitefield's hearers at Philadelphia were exaggerations (Franklin, *op. cit.*, pp. 129–33). Yet these reports are to be regarded as rough estimates. Friends of the movement might easily in perfect honesty overestimate the number. The published statements probably came from them, as we know was the case in the beginning when Seward was the traveling companion of Whitefield.

[3] *Pennsylvania Gazette*, November 8, 1739.   [4] *Ibid.*

[5] Boston *News-Letter*, November 30, 1739.

[6] Whitefield, *Journal*, No. 5, pp. 27–29, 47.

friend and supporter.[1] He had fraternal intercourse with the Swedish minister and received repeated courtesies from Commissary Cummings.[2] The commissary was a politic man, very different from the combative Vesey, of New York, as both were different from the strong and evangelical Blair, of Williamsburg. For all this it must not be supposed for a moment that Whitefield was dumb upon a conviction which was burned into his very soul. He believed that the people could not be brought to embrace the truth until they were convinced that they had been falsely led. Therefore Jonathan Allen, the church missionary, took great offense when the young preacher asserted at Philadelphia that the majority of Anglican ministers did not preach the truth, making them wolves in sheep's clothing.[3] In a dissenting meeting-house he would have condemned the body of dissenting ministers, but it was classes, not individuals, that he branded as unconverted.

The ministerial intercourse which most delighted the young preacher, now in his twenty-fifth year, was that with the old, gray-headed William Tennent, of Neshaminy. Whitefield says in his journal that Tennent was a great friend of the Erskines, and just as they were hated by the judicatories of the Church of Scotland, and as his Methodist associates were despised by their brethren of the Church of England, so too were Tennent and his sons treated by the majority of the synod. But just as surely as Elijah overcame the prophets of Baal, so would the few evangelicals overcome their opposers, thought Whitefield. The aged founder of the Log College had made the journey of twenty miles from Neshaminy, called by the voice of spiritual kinship, and the result was an alliance between Whitefield, chief exponent of storm and stress in religion, Anglican though he was, and the New Brunswick Presbyterians, who above all others had made the Middle Colonies ready for a religious revolution.[4]

After nine days at Philadelphia, Whitefield journeyed toward New York, preaching at Burlington, the old capital of West Jersey, and at New Brunswick, the home of Gilbert Tennent.[5] In the company of riders was Jonathan Allen, the clerical itinerant already mentioned. He bitterly attacked the Calvinism of Whitefield and rebuked him for publicly condemning the dead Tillotson and the living bishops and clergy. Whitefield's recourse was to pronounce him a carnal man unable to

---

[1] *Ibid.*, p. 28.   [2] *Ibid.*, pp. 29, 31.

[3] *Ibid.*, p. 32; Boston *News-Letter*, November 30, 1739.

[4] Whitefield, *Journal*, No. 5, p. 31.   [5] *Ibid.*, p. 34.

discern the things of the Spirit.[1]   Possibly restrained by the chastisement which he had received on the way to New Brunswick, Whitefield excuses every slight divergence from the usages of his church.   There was at that time no place in New Brunswick set apart for the worship of the Church of England.   But learning that it was the custom of the country for dissenters and conformists to worship at different times in the same building, he accepted the invitation of Gilbert Tennent to preach in his meeting-house.   It was none the less an Anglican service, for the liturgy was used.[2]   The remaining miles to New York were short ones, for Whitefield and Tennent cheered each other by the relation of their similar struggles and victories.

The travelers were welcomed at New York by an influential layman who had twice invited Whitefield to visit the city.   With this gentleman and Seward, his traveling companion, the evangelist called upon Commissary Vesey, but the interview was a stormy one.   The use of the church was denied.   Vesey charged Whitefield with breaking the canons, and Whitefield returned the charge, for he had been informed that Vesey was a frequenter of taverns.[3]   Vesey, a graduate of Harvard, had come to Long Island as a dissenting minister.   Indeed as such he was elected minister in New York, but the wily Governor Fletcher had already won him over to the Anglican communion.   Having been imposed upon an overwhelmingly dissenting population by a trick, he remained a clerical politician.   The unscrupulous Cornbury was a governor after his heart, but milder governors were bitterly opposed by Vesey.[4]   Such was the man who had listened to the story of Jonathan Allen and abetted him in his newspaper war upon Whitefield.

Allen followed Whitefield up, determined to dispute with him. Whitefield was just at that time the guest of William Smith, a Presbyterian and a leading lawyer, one of the few college graduates in the province and father of its future historian.   Smith lent himself so far to the purposes of Allen that he invited him to his table.   Here Allen violated the laws of hospitality, so abusive was he of Whitefield, who refused to enter into disputation with him.[5]   Thereupon Allen published several letters against Whitefield, remarkable for their billingsgate.   In them he urged the people to treat with neglect and contempt the pre-

---

[1] New York *Post-Boy*, January 21, 1745.

[2] Whitefield, *Journal*, No. 5, p. 35.   [3] *Ibid.*, p. 36.

[4] *Eccl. Rec. of New York*, p. 2016; Briggs, *American Presbyterianism*, pp. 108, 144, 145.

[5] Boston *Evening Post*, February 11, 1740.

tender to divine inspiration.[1] He also turned upon his host, William Smith, making him a deceiver. Then Smith replied in measured judicial language but clearly proved Whitefield to have shown himself the gentleman, and Allen the ruffian.[2] Whitefield did not reply in public print, and his journals make not the slightest allusion to Allen. Others came to the defense of the evangelist, among them Mangus Falconer, a New Side of Philadelphia, and wielder of an acrid pen.[3] These letters, pro and con, were copied from one paper to another, and so the debate attained the proportions of an intercolonial controversy occupying the public mind from Boston to Charleston.

On the evening of Whitefield's arrival at New York he listened to a sermon preached by Gilbert Tennent in the Presbyterian Church. Never before had he heard such a searching discourse.[4] The polished Oxford graduate was taking lessons in the art of effective oratory from the rough product of the Log College. So deeply was he moved by the truth, as he considered it, presented by his new friend and by the evident success of a method so overwhelming and so terribly direct that his own method of preaching was sensibly changed by his intercourse with the Tennents. When he visited New York again, early the next year, a roughness was noticed by his hearers which was said to have been lately acquired.[5] Just as his Calvinism was stiffened by his intercourse with Presbyterians, so, fully conscious of his youth and inexperience, he was ever ready to learn from men whose piety and success commanded his admiration.

With the pulpit of Trinity Church closed to Whitefield he applied for the use of the Dutch church, but Domine Boel, the antagonist of Frelinghuysen, refused him.[6] Pemberton, of the Presbyterian church, offered the use of his meeting-house, but Whitefield was slow to accept it because of the bitterness between Anglicans and Presbyterians.[7] Under the governorship of Cornbury, Presbyterians had been persecuted in New York, and even now their congregation in the city was unable to obtain a charter. Whitefield, lest he should appear as the spokesman of a party and his influence be restricted to its following, resorted in New York to field preaching. A long, sympathetic account of his activities

---

[1] Boston *News-Letter*, November 30, 1739; *American Weekly Mercury*, January 10, 1740; New York *Gazette*, January 22, 1740; New York *Post-Boy*, January 21, 1745.

[2] *American Weekly Mercury*, December 13, 1739.

[3] *Ibid.*, December 6, 1739.

[4] Whitefield, *Journal*, No. 5, p. 35.

[5] Boston *News-Letter*, June 5, 1740.

[6] *Eccl. Rec. of New York*, p. 2798.

[7] Whitefield, *Journal*, No. 5, p. 37.

was contributed to a New York paper, and this was copied by others. With a deft pen Mr. Pemberton, for the article was attributed to him, described Whitefield's preaching from a little eminence to a great multitude disposed upon the descent before him and on either side. There were two companies, a compact body of people who hung upon his words, and an encircling assembly whose laughter and scoffing aroused the speaker to subdue these "vassals of the devil." He succeeded, for a solemn awe fell upon the whole assembly, and the author of the description was astonished at what he saw and felt. Every scruple vanished, and he confessed that he had never seen or heard the like.[1]

Whitefield consented to preach in the Presbyterian meeting-house when he learned that even Mr. Vesey had preached in the Dutch Reformed. He did so in the evening, following his afternoon sermon in the fields, and he continued to speak there twice a day in addition to the daily preaching in the fields. The outdoor assemblies increased in spite of the cold November air. On Sunday morning he preached at eight o'clock in the meeting-house and from thence went to Trinity Church to hear his doctrines assailed. At the close of the day, in the meeting-house, the windows of which were removed to permit the throng outside to hear, he retorted by cautioning the people against the scribes and Pharisees of his own communion. Thousands had come to hear his farewell sermon.[2] In four days he had won a great popular following. In a city where deep religious emotion was almost unknown Whitefield by his frankness, earnestness, and pathos had opened a fountain of tears. Great was the lamentation of the people at his going.

On the return journey toward Philadelphia Whitefield accepted the previously given invitation of Jonathan Dickinson, Presbyterian pastor at Elizabethtown. In his sermon the young enthusiast did not fail to "open his mouth" against both ministers and people among the dissenters who contented themselves with a bare, speculative knowledge of the doctrines of grace, "never experiencing the power of them in their hearts."[3] Dickinson had not previously entered into cordial relations with Gilbert Tennent. Whitefield's journal does not show the warmth of fraternal feeling toward the theologian which he always expresses when recording his intercourse with ministers of the New Brunswick party. But Dickinson was sincerely evangelical, and this invitation to the most prominent exponent of revivalism thoroughly committed him

[1] *American Weekly Mercury*, December 27, 1739; *Christian History* for 1744, p. 359.

[2] Whitefield, *Journal*, No. 5, p. 39.   [3] *Ibid.*, p. 40.

to it. At the same time the commendation given to Whitefield by Pemberton contributed to a union in evangelistic endeavor between the presbytery of New York and the more radical New Brunswick party.

Coming again to New Brunswick the evangelist met several of the leaders of the evangelical movement in the Middle Colonies. Among them was Domine Frelinghuysen, whom Whitefield calls "the beginner of the great work in these parts."[1] Another was John Cross, Presbyterian pastor at Basking Ridge. The members of his hill congregation were called "enthusiasts and mad men" by those who were ignorant of the hidden Christ-life, reports Whitefield. Still another was James Campbell, of Newtown, Pennsylvania, a neighbor of the elder Tennent. Campbell, under distress of soul from the conviction that he was unconverted, had ceased to preach, but Whitefield persuaded him to resume preaching and expressed his belief that the new unction of the preacher would convict many hypocrites among the dissenting ministers.[2]

At Maidenhead Whitefield preached from a wagon to a great assembly gathered from the surrounding country. Here he met John Rowland, of whose success he speaks approvingly.[3] At Trenton, the next point on the way toward Philadelphia, he preached in the courthouse in the presence of a condemned criminal, but no mention is made of David Cowel, Presbyterian pastor at Trenton, leader of the conservatives in those parts. At Neshaminy he found a crowd gathered from far and wide, which he estimated at three thousand.[4] He describes the log house, in contempt called the college. To his mind it resembled the schools of the old prophets. Carnal ministers, according to Whitefield, opposed the venerable teacher because his faithful preachers drew the people away from their ministry.[5] At Abington, near Philadelphia, the traveler preached to another throng, speaking from a window of the meeting-house. Richard Treat was pastor here. So deeply affected was Treat by the pathetic appeal of the evangelist that he concluded he was himself a stranger to grace. He attempted to preach, but could not, and confessed to his people how he had deceived them and himself.

---

[1] *Ibid.*, p. 41.   [2] *Ibid.*, p. 42.

[3] *Ibid.*, p. 43.

[4] *Ibid.*, p. 45: "It is surprizing how such Bodies of People so scattered abroad, can be gathered at so short a Warning. I believe at Neshamonie there might be near a thousand Horses." Yet in the Kentucky Revival of 1801 some wilderness congregations were estimated at the time from eighteen to twenty-five thousand. Cleveland, *The Great Revival in the West*, p. 75.

[5] Whitefield, *Journal*, No. 5, p. 44.

Nevertheless he continued to preach, sorrowing, in the hope that assurance would be granted him.[1]

After these triumphs in three provinces Whitefield returned to Philadelphia. The enthusiasm of the people mounted higher and higher. It was estimated that his congregation at Germantown numbered five thousand people, and that his farewell sermon at Philadelphia had ten thousand hearers.[2] With the exception of these two meetings in the open air his twice-daily preaching services were in the church. After five stirring days he left Philadelphia, accompanied by one hundred and fifty horsemen, stopping and preaching at various points until he reached White Clay Creek, the home of Charles Tennent. Whitefield's appointments had been well advertised, for the number of his hearers far exceeded those of his journey across New Jersey.[3] This region had been longer settled, and the population was greater. Charles Tennent was a less gifted brother of Gilbert, but he was an ardent supporter of the evangelical cause in a region where opposers were numerous. Another Presbyterian minister of that region who assured Whitefield of his good will was George Gillespie, of Christiana.

Upon entering Maryland there was an abrupt change in the size of the audiences as reported in the papers. No longer were the hearers of the evangelist computed by thousands. This was true of the long journey through the coast district where "roads were very bad," till he reached Charleston and later distant Savannah.

A very just representation of the effect of this first journey of Whitefield through the Middle Colonies was published in the *South Carolina Gazette:* "We hear from Philadelphia and New York that since Mr. Whitefield's preaching in those places several week-day lectures have been set up, which are much crowded, and that sermons, which used to be the greatest drug, are now the only books in demand."[4] The advertising columns of the papers substantiate this statement, for the sudden output of religious books was astonishing, especially of Whitefield's sermons and journals and the Wesleys' hymns. That the effects of Whitefield's ministry in Philadelphia were more than a passing wave of emotion is shown by the establishment of daily religious services which were continued for over a year, and of meetings of the same char-

[1] Whitefield, *Journal*, No. 6, p. 20.

[2] *Pennsylvania Gazette*, November 29, 1739.

[3] *Virginia Gazette*, January 18, 1740.

[4] *South Carolina Gazette*, March 15, 1740.

acter three times on Sunday.   Twenty-six associations for prayer were formed.[1]   For the future religious life of the country there was even greater significance in the alliance of this young priest of the Church of England with the extreme evangelical party within the Presbyterian Church.   The witchery of Whitefield's oratory and the prestige of his name were given to the Tennents in their struggle against formality and lifelessness in the church.

[1] Webster, *A History of the Presbyterian Church*, p. 165.

CHAPTER V

THE YEAR 1740, THE GREAT AWAKENING AT HIGH TIDE

The Great Awakening is often called the revival of 1740,[1] for that was the year of Whitefield's journey through New England, a year when New England turned from religious indifference to a quickened interest as great as animated the founders of the commonwealth of Massachusetts. It was also the year of high tide in the religious excitement throughout the Middle Colonies. The two journeys of Whitefield and the meeting of the Presbyterian synod divide the year into five parts.

1. *Progress of the revival before the spring tour of Whitefield.*—This period embraces the first three and a half months of the year. It was during this time that the revival at Newark, New Jersey, attained its height, "when the whole town in general was brought under an uncommon concern about their eternal interests." This revival had begun among the young people in August, 1739, as noted in the preceding chapter. As late as February, 1741—for we must sum up the work at Newark in a single paragraph—the interest was still intense, when "the greatest concern appeared among the risen generation." Yet at no time was there a special preaching of terror. The convicted did indeed cry out in agony, but Burr, and Dickinson, who came to Burr's assistance, strove to repress excessive emotionalism. In spite of their efforts to avoid just cause of censure a spirit of censoriousness did appear among some of the new converts. This and other blemishes, almost inseparable from religious excitement, aroused opposition at Newark, even among some who had acknowledged a beneficent and mysterious power as working mightily in their midst.[2]

The general but smoldering religious fire burst into flame at other points in that section of the country. There was a revival during the spring of 1740 in the highlands of New York under Leonard, of Goshen, and William Tennent, Jr., went to his assistance.[3] In the same province

---

[1] Edwards, *Thoughts on the Revival of Religion in New England in 1740;* Tracy, *The Great Awakening*, p. iii of Preface.

[2] *Christian History* for 1743, pp. 252–54.

[3] Whitefield, *Journal*, No. 6, p. 30; Webster, *A History of the Presbyterian Church*, p. 458.

at the eastern extremity of Long Island James Davenport went forth like the Hebrew prince with his armor bearer against the Philistines. Davenport was in his twenty-fourth year, and Barber, his assistant, was his college classmate. Under them "lasting good was done" at Easthampton, but their methods were so fantastic that people not in sympathy with the itinerants thought them mad.[1] Dickinson, Burr, Leonard, Davenport, and Barber were all Yale men, and, Dickinson excepted, all were of about Whitefield's age.

At the same time that numerous communities in New Jersey and New York, notably Maidenhead, Newark, Goshen, and Easthampton, were highly excited over frequent and startling convictions and conversions, a more surprising outburst of the same spirit occurred in the very stronghold of Scotch-Irish conservatism, the southwestern Pennsylvanian settlements of that day. It began in the congregation of Samuel Blair at Fagg's Manor.[2] The sermons of Blair were directed principally to the unregenerate and were very searching. In March, 1740, he was returning from a fortnight's absence in New Jersey, when a hundred miles away from home a message reached him that a "deep soul concern" had appeared among his people. The fame of the revival soon attracted people from afar. Blair frequently exhorted his hearers to moderate their passions without stifling their convictions. The greater part silently wept, but some were overcome and fainted. He could not condemn as spurious the experiences of those who were the subjects of unusual bodily motions. Yet there were a few who, seeing others weep and faint, endeavored to be affected in the same way; their bodily agitations did not come from a sense of unworthiness, or even from terror at the displeasure of Jehovah. Blair gives a careful analysis of the cases which came under his observation.[3]

Members of other congregations who had flocked to Fagg's Manor carried the revival spirit back to their respective communities. One of these towns was Nottingham, twenty miles from Fagg's Manor, a vacancy[4] in the presbytery of Donegal. This presbytery was the center of opposition to the revival. Only two of its ministers, Creaghead and

[1] Whitefield, *Journal*, No. 6, p. 32; Webster, *op. cit.*, p. 536.

[2] Blair had removed from Shrewsbury, New Jersey, to Fagg's Manor, Pennsylvania, in 1739. He was the second Log College man to join the presbytery of New Castle, Charles Tennent having preceded him. MS Minutes of the New Brunswick Presbytery for July 31, September 5, October 11, 1739.

[3] *Christian History* for 1744, pp. 242–60.

[4] A pastorless congregation.

Alexander, were favorable to it.   The revival at Nottingham in the midst of hostile territory began under the preaching there of Samuel Blair, and he was followed by the Tennents, and even by John Cross.[1] There was a party of opposition within the church, and Cross was denied the use of the meeting-house.   Other vacancies from time to time were supplied by New Side ministers upon the invitation of the people.   Sometimes pastors who were unfriendly to the movement yielded to the importunities of their parishioners and invited these itinerating evangelists into their pulpits.[2]   Preaching under such circumstances was not intrusion.   It was not a violation of synodical rules.

On March 8, 1740, Gilbert Tennent preached his famous Nottingham sermon on the "Danger of an Unconverted Ministry."   It was a terrible arraignment of men who entered the ministry as a trade, and who, though approved by the public institutions of learning and regularly admitted by the ecclesiastical authorities, were strangers to a consuming religious zeal.   Unconverted themselves, they were unconcerned, though many years passed without a conversion in their congregations. Yet in a day of quickened interest they raised their voices against the frenzied preachers, as they represented them to be, who by uncharitable methods put poor people out of their wits.   These Pharisees of his day resembled those of old, thought Tennent, "as one crow's egg does another."   He advised his hearers, who were gathered from many congregations of the Donegal presbytery, to frequent the meetings of preachers from whom they received the greatest benefit, each applying, however, first to his own pastor for his consent.[3]   No names were mentioned, but every minister recognized by his people as hostile to Whitefield, Tennent, and the revival interpreted the sermon as an attack upon himself.   The popular mind was decidedly favorable to the revival, and these opposing ministers—a number of them assuredly—were brave men who lifted their voices against what they imagined to be dangerous tendencies.   Many of them lost the more active and spiritual from their congregations.   They attributed their losses to the instigation of this and similar discourses.   The Nottingham sermon, which was repeatedly published and widely circulated, was one of the causes of the disruption of the Presbyterian Church, but its ultimate effect was to make its doctrine the dominant policy of that church.[4]

[1] Whitefield, *Journal*, No. 6, p. 43.

[2] *Christian History* for 1744, pp. 260, 261, 297.

[3] Gilbert Tennent, *The Danger of an Unconverted Ministry*.

[4] Gledstone, *George Whitefield*, p. 122.

2. *The spring tour of Whitefield.*—We have just seen how full advantage was taken of the impetus given by Whitefield to a religious reformation. Now he was coming again to lend the good cause the magnetism of his presence, but we shall presently discover another side, the humanitarian, of this many-sided movement. Whitefield's second evangelistic journey through the Middle Colonies was made in the spring of 1740. He landed at New Castle, Delaware, on April 13, and sailed from Lewes on May 25. It was now that he made his appeals in behalf of his orphan house.[1] Georgia was itself established as a charity, but the distressed from the Old World, as a critic of Whitefield put it, had found their graves in the New World. Georgia "turned out to be to them the severest cruelty." They "died in numbers, leaving their helpless babes quite destitute, and in a wilderness; so that out of the ruins of this first charitable project, sprang up grounds for a second, that of an orphan house."[2] Whitefield from the first proclaimed that he founded his orphan house upon the model of the famous one at Halle. He intended to make it part of an evangelistic and educational propaganda. He was encouraged by what he saw of the diminutive orphan house established by the Salzburgers in Georgia, and by his intercourse with the Moravians, who sustained a similar enterprise at Herrnhut, Saxony. Though Bethesda, as he called his orphan house, has an honorable name in the early history of Georgia, its greater significance is that it furnished the occasion of its young founder preaching in every American province.[3] In a cold, unsympathetic age he awakened the mellowing and civilizing emotions, so that men had a strange, new passion for their fellows, as well as a new delight in their God.

Still other philanthropic enterprises were contemplated by Whitefield at this time. Through his whole life his boundless humanity and inextinguishable enthusiasm led him to establish, or at least, actively assist, all manner of benevolences. When he had made his first long journey through the southern provinces he published an address to the planters on behalf of the oppressed slaves. He wrote like an Old Testament prophet stirred by the wrongs of the poor. It was not the institution of slavery which he attacked but its abuse. He asked that the negroes be treated humanely and, most important of all, be instructed in the principles of the Christian religion.[4] Men like Commissary Garden, of Charleston, criticized the address as an incitement to insurrection,[5]

[1] Whitefield, *Journal*, No. 5, p. 48.   [2] Boston *Evening Post*, November 19, 1744.
[3] Whitefield, *Journal*, No. 6, p. 46.
[4] *New England Weekly Journal*, April 29, 1740.
[5] Garden, *Six Letters to the Reverend G. Whitefield*, pp. 145–50.

but it did not cost Whitefield his popularity in South Carolina.   Published in many of the papers, it was the one strong appeal in that time in the interest of the negro, and it turned the newly awakened sympathies of Christian people to the extension of a helping hand to the African in America.

Two projects illustrative of this new attitude to the black man were planned by Whitefield at this time.   Even though the primary purpose of this journey was the collection of funds for Bethesda, the forlorn state of the negroes in the North, as well as in the South, made him cry out in their behalf and led him to the resolution to found schools for them in Philadelphia and at the Forks of the Delaware.   He actually set up the school in Philadelphia with the former dancing-master as teacher.[1] The other project was more ambitious.   At the Forks of the Delaware, near Easton, he purchased a manor of five thousand acres on which to establish a negro school.   To this tract he gave the name of Nazareth, which it still bears.   It was intended not only as a charity for negroes but also as a refuge for oppressed English Methodists.[2]   The erection of the school building at Nazareth was committed to the Moravians, and the wealthy William Seward, who had already purchased a sloop and lent it to Whitefield, now advanced the purchase money for the Nazareth tract.   Seward's sudden death obliged Whitefield to sell the manor to the Moravians, who had in the meantime purchased the neighboring tract of Bethlehem.   The dedication of Nazareth to education and religion was splendidly fulfilled by the Moravians, though not in the specific form that was intended by the first great friend of the American negro.[3]

The second journey was, however, no less evangelistic than the first.   It is not necessary to follow his itinerary, for he traveled along the same highways between the two leading cities as the year before, except that a greater number of side excursions were made.   Instead we shall study his relations with the various denominations of Christians and first with his fellow churchmen.   Commissary Cummings took umbrage at Whitefield's strictures upon the latitudinarian teachings of Archbishop Tillotson and ostensibly upon this ground denied Whitefield the use of Christ Church.   Furthermore the commissary complained that the press of the city was shut up against opposers.[4]   Franklin denied the truth of

[1] Boston *News-Letter*, August 21, 1740.

[2] Franklin, *Autobiography*, p. 130; *New England Weekly Journal*, May 6, 20, June 3, 1740.

[3] J. T. Hamilton, *The Moravian Church in the United States*, p. 439.

[4] Whitefield, *Journal*, No. 6, p. 19; *Pennsylvania Gazette*, April 10, 1740.

the report that Whitefield had engaged all the printers to suppress criticism upon him.[1] The philosopher-printer became the lifelong friend and admirer of the evangelist.[2] The favor of the three papers reflected the state of public opinion. Now that the Church of England was closed to Whitefield he preached twice a day in the open to crowds which the church could never have held.

One evening he went to the Baptist meeting-house to hear Jenkin Jones, the pastor, of whom he said, reporting the sermon, "He is the only preacher that I know of in Philadelphia who speaks feelingly and with authority."[3] Afterward Whitefield preached at the Baptist meeting-house at Pennypack to a great throng. He speaks of Abel Morgan as one sent forth in this day of grace to preach with wonderful unction.[4] A denomination which was insignificant in Whitefield's day and sadly divided was receiving its baptism of power, which subsequently made it a mighty force in the religious life of the nation.

In the preceding year the Germans of Pennsylvania had received the young orator as if he were Spener or Francke come to life again. We have already seen how he was associated with the Moravians in the founding of Nazareth in the present year. Now he preached at some of the German settlements in the interior and noted with admiration the simplicity and fervor of their worship. Peter Boehler, in these German meetings, was both interpreter and assistant.[5] This Moravian missionary, now described by Whitefield as a dear lover of the Lord, had been the instructor of John Wesley in his search for a personal experience similar to what he so admired in the Moravians. Some hostile critics later said that Whitefield brought swarms of Moravians to the Middle Colonies. He did give passage to a little company of them when they abandoned their mission in stricken Georgia and came on his sloop to New Castle.[6] He later broke with them over doctrinal questions, but his heart was too genial and his sympathy too broad to allow him long to be at variance with so good a people. Whitefield and the Moravians fanned the spirit of Pietism again into flame among the German immigrants.

The Dutch of New Jersey and New York were also stirred by the visits of Whitefield in 1739 and 1740. The greatest of the revivals under Frelinghuysen was now in progress. In our account of the contest within the Dutch Reformed Church reference was made to the stage

---

[1] *Ibid.*, May 8, 1740.

[2] Franklin, *op. cit.*, p. 132.

[3] Whitefield, *Journal*, No. 6, p. 35.

[4] *Ibid.*, p. 36.

[5] *Ibid.*, p. 26.

[6] Hamilton, *op. cit.*, p. 439.

erected for Whitefield at New York, whereon sat Domines DuBois and
Frelinghuysen, one the most influential of Dutch pastors and the other
the leader of the reforming party.   It was at this time that Whitefield
accepted the invitation of Domine Freeman to preach in his church at
Flatbush.   Thus the evangelist joined with the party of Frelinghuysen
to extend the revival among the Dutch,[1] with what ultimate results
will be told in a later chapter.

It must always be remembered that while the great popular following
of Whitefield included numerous representatives of every denomination,
even of Quakers and Anglicans, yet the chief interest lies in the contest
within the Presbyterian Church.   The most active itinerants resident
in these colonies were Presbyterians, and soon the most outspoken
critics of the Great Awakening were to be of this communion.   At
Woodbridge on this journey Whitefield preached for John Pierson, thus
further drawing the presbytery of New York into union with the presbytery of New Brunswick.   But the meetings which exceeded all others in
the absence of restraint upon the emotions were held at Nottingham and
Fagg's Manor, where the New Brunswick men had brought feeling to
high tension.   As the orator, quickly responsive to the sympathetic
atmosphere, spoke out of the fulness of his love, certain of the auditors
fainted, revived, listened, and fainted again.   In the midst of such
scenes at Fagg's Manor an opposer, a member of the synod, challenged
Whitefield to public disputation.   There was no appreciable doctrinal
difference between the debaters, except that Whitefield urged Christians
to seek assurance, while his critic would leave them in a state of uncer-
tainty.   The real meaning of the incident was that opposition to revivalism now became outspoken.   It was the answer of the conservative
Presbyterians to Gilbert Tennent's Nottingham sermon.   In Whitefield's
farewell sermon at Philadelphia, preached to a greater throng than he
had ever before faced in America, he recommended to his hearers the
Tennents and their associates as most worthy preachers.[2]

3. *The meeting of the synod.*—Three days after Whitefield preached
his last sermon at Lewes, Delaware, the synod of Philadelphia met.   The
act concerning presbyterial bounds had been trampled under foot by a
priest of the Church of England and by the Presbyterian pastors and
congregations that had invited him to their pulpits.   The synod yielded
to the demand for the repeal of the measure, declaring that it "heartily
rejoiced in the labors of the ministry in other places besides their own
particular charge," and now agreed that ministers should "conduct

---

[1] Whitefield, *Journal*, No. 6, pp. 30, 31.   [2] *Ibid.*, p. 39.

themselves as though it had never been."[1] This is the language of conciliation and was part of an intended healing measure.

A compromise, satisfactory to neither side, was also reached dealing with the anomalous position of the probationers and ministers of the New Brunswick presbytery who had not submitted to synodical examination. In the language of the overture "the synod declared that they do not thereby call in question the power of subordinate presbyteries to ordain ministers but only assert their own right to judge of the qualifications of their own members." They therefore acknowledge men in the position of Rowland to be "truly gospel ministers," but they refuse to admit them to the synod till they have fulfilled its requirements. The synod consents, however, "that they be in all other respects treated and considered as ministers of the gospel, anything that may be otherwise construed in any of our former proceedings notwithstanding."[2]

When Gilbert Tennent had wrested from the majority the repeal of a measure which was intended to restrict the operations of the New Brunswick ministers and had vindicated the assertion by that presbytery of its scriptural and historical rights, as represented in Presbyterian directories and treatises, he might well have left to the future the complete victory of the Log College party. But the pugnacity of his race, highly developed by a life of contention, did not permit him to accept from the majority anything less than absolute surrender. Thrilled by the thought that the day of opportunity had come to the church for effective evangelistic labor when the public mind was aroused to the importance of religion, he could not understand why ministers held back. He felt that their insistence upon synodical authority, their exaltation of order, and their fear of an uneducated ministry were all masks to cover their hatred of vital religion. Therefore he wrote a terrific indictment of his fellow members of the synod who had taken the stand against the movement. Samuel Blair wrote another not so passionate but no less offensive. The synod listened to the reading of these papers in the presence of a great congregation which sympathized with the position taken by the writers. If Tennent and Blair aimed to convince their opposers they had taken an unfortunate course. If their purpose was to incite them to disorderly measures in retaliation they had succeeded. Thus ended the meeting of the synod with the majority exasperated and indignant.[3]

[1] *Records of the Presbyterian Church*, p. 152.

[2] *Ibid.*, p. 152.

[3] Hodge, *Constitutional History of the Presbyterian Church*, Part II, p. 120.

4. *Progress of the revival from the meeting of the synod to the autumn tour of Whitefield.*—While Jonathan Dickinson and other advocates of conciliation were endeavoring in synod to formulate measures of peace between the extreme reactionaries and the belligerent advocates of revivalism, Gilbert Tennent and his associates were interested less in the proceedings of the synod than in the great meetings held on Society Hill, Philadelphia. During the five days' session fourteen sermons were preached by the Tennents and Samuel Blair and by two preachers who were not members of the synod, James Davenport, of Southold, Long Island, and John Rowland. There were other special services in the Presbyterian and Baptist meeting-houses and expoundings and exhortations in private houses according to the custom of Whitefield. The alteration was said to be surprising. Never before had the people shown greater willingness to attend preaching services, nor the preachers greater zeal in their office. Religion was the one interest of the time.[1]

Some of the New Side evangelists were detained in the city by the clamor of the people after the adjournment of the synod. On the Sunday following, Gilbert Tennent preached four times, twice on Society Hill, once in the Presbyterian meeting-house, and once in the Baptist. His largest audience was estimated at eight thousand. Rowland preached twice in the Baptist meeting-house. At one of these services the people were so overcome by his description of the undone condition of sinners that Tennent went to the pulpit stairs and cried out, "Oh, Brother Rowland, is there no balm in Gilead?" Then the speaker, startled by the effect upon his hearers of his fearful words, began to unfold the way of recovery.[2] Tennent refers to this emotional power of Rowland, which was sometimes too little restrained, when in his funeral sermon he says: "Being young in years, and of a warm temper, he was thereby led into some indiscretions in his honest and earnest attempts to do good, which it pleased God to convince him of and reclaim him from a considerable time before his last remove."[3]

The criticism of Rowland was not all so kindly. Jenkin Jones, the pastor of the Baptist churches at Philadelphia and Pennypack, was a warm friend of the revival, though he shared Tennent's desire to curb any excess of emotionalism among the people. His assistant, Ebenezer Kinnersly, subsequently a professor in the University of Pennsylvania, had no patience with emotional demonstrations. In the absence of

[1] Boston *News-Letter*, June 26, July 31, 1740.
[2] Webster, *op. cit.*, p. 471.
[3] Gilbert Tennent, *A Funeral Sermon . . . . Rev. John Rowland*, p. 42.

the pastor he bitterly condemned the sermons of Rowland. He said that the people were terrified to distraction, driven to despair, or filled with enthusiastic raptures. The speaker's characterization of Rowland's method was so resented by his hearers that many left the building. Charges were made against Kinnersly in church meeting, and he was temporarily barred from communion. The abusive letter which he wrote, for the publication of which Franklin apologized to the public,[1] was itself a severe censure upon the conduct of Kinnersly,[2] but there was doubtless some basis for his objections to the unregulated emotionalism which sometimes attended the impassioned oratory of Rowland.

The progress of events takes us back to the neighborhood of Newark, where the revival early in the year had been so remarkable. It is to be recalled that Jonathan Dickinson joined in that work and invited Whitefield into his own pulpit. Dickinson now reports a remarkable manifestation of the divine presence at Elizabethtown, beginning in June of that year. A sudden and deep impression came upon the people, but there was no crying out or falling down, though there were audible sobbing and sighing in all parts of the assembly. The work here, as at Newark, began among the young people, but persons of all ages were reached. Conversions were not sudden, for converts were a long time under "law-work." This was usual among Calvinists. When the consciousness of God's love burst upon the converts there were no ecstatic raptures, such as had been reported in some places. The number reached by this movement is suggested by a passage in a private letter in which Dickinson says, "I have had more young people address me for direction in their spiritual concern within these three months than in thirty years before."[3]

The presbytery of New Brunswick, not the presbytery of New York, was the center of evangelizing itinerancy. We must therefore trace its activities in sending out laborers to the white fields, and, this done, we must follow its leading member in his greatest successes. James McCrea accepted the call of a group of congregations newly constituted within the bounds of the presbytery.[4] William Robinson, who possessed an attractive and amiable personality and later attained great success in Virginia, was sent to a group of churches formerly served by Samuel Blair. Samuel Finley, a man who combined the scholarship of Blair and the disputatious spirit and preaching power of Gilbert Tennent, was

[1] *Pennsylvania Gazette*, July 24, 1740.   [2] *Ibid.*, October 9, 1740.

[3] *Christian History* for 1743, pp. 254–58.

[4] MS Minutes of the New Brunswick Presbytery for April 1, 1740.

licensed to preach as a probationer wherever Providence might direct. He went to Nottingham in the presbytery of Donegal. His presence there was most annoying to the Old Side ministers of that conservative presbytery.

The late summer and early autumn were devoted by Gilbert Tennent to a two months' journey "southward" through the destitute regions of what is now called South Jersey, a tour that was extended even to Maryland.[1] Samuel Blair had previously itinerated in the same region. In the whole extent of country from Gloucester, near Philadelphia, to Cape May there were in 1740 but two pastors, Elmer, of Fairfield, and Evans, of Piles Grove, both Old Side ministers. In this region a number of ancient churches sent out a feeble cry for help.[2] Whitefield, after his autumn tour, reported the singular power of Tennent's meetings at Cohansey and Salem.[3] The success of both Tennent and Whitefield in this region was apparently greatest at Greenwich in Cohansey, where the New Side interest was afterward strong. Aided now and later by the New Brunswick presbytery, new life was given to the South Jersey churches. They continued prosperous until the Revolutionary War.[4] Just what churches were visited by Gilbert Tennent in Delaware and Maryland is not recorded, but they probably included the churches of Charles Tennent, Gillespie, and Hutchinson, who were friends of the revival and reported a great reformation in some of the congregations in those parts.[5]

The success of this evangelistic journey immediately became a decisive factor when a larger opportunity was presented. When Whitefield entered the Middle Colonies again after his astonishing triumph in New England and Tennent returned from his "southward" journey, the two itinerants held a conference at New Brunswick. Whitefield was accompanied by Daniel Rogers, tutor in Harvard College and a recent convert. Rogers brought to Tennent an invitation from several prominent ministers of New England to visit Boston and New England in general for the extension of the religious interest so powerfully awakened by Whitefield. Tennent was distrustful but was persuaded by

[1] *New England Weekly Journal*, January 27, 1741.

[2] Brown, *History of the Presbyterian Churches in West or South Jersey*, pp. 10–14.

[3] Whitefield, *Journal*, No. 7, p. 74.

[4] Brown, *op. cit.*, pp. 20, 24.

[5] Gillespie, *A Letter to the . . . . Presbytery of New York*, p. 7; Whitefield, *Journal*, No. 7, p. 61.

Whitefield and other friends and encouraged by his late success to under-take the mission.[1]

Tennent went to Boston with Rogers, and for three months, accord-ing to the hostile Dr. Cutler, "people wallowed in the snow for the benefit of his beastly brayings."[2] His dress and personality were ridi-culed, but nearly all of the pastors, and the most eminent of them, testi-fied to the power of his preaching. The results exceeded those under the preaching of Whitefield. Nothing so wonderful had ever been witnessed in Boston,[3] and there were similar results in many other places. When he preached at New Haven a number of the students were con-verted. Several of these entered the Presbyterian ministry in the Middle Colonies. Among them was James Sprout, for twenty-four years pastor of the church later established by Gilbert Tennent in Phila-delphia.[4] Tennent left home in November, 1740, and he returned just before the meeting of the synod in 1741.

5. *The autumn tour of Whitefield.*—Repeated reference has been made to the triumphal progress of Whitefield through New England. He landed at Newport, Rhode Island, on September 14, 1740, entered the Middle Colonies at Rye, New York, on October 29, and sailed from Reedy Island in the Delaware Bay on December 1. He traveled more than eight hundred miles in this autumn through New England and the Middle Colonies and collected a sum in excess of seven hundred pounds sterling.[5]

His experiences in the Middle Colonies were like those of his two earlier journeys. There was no diminution of his popularity. His route was little changed from that taken before. At Rye he was invited by the rector to preach in the English church, an encouraging sign that his own church was not wholly unsympathetic with an evangelical reformation. At Trenton he was invited by the Old Side Presbyterian minister, Cowell, to preach in his meeting-house, an indication that all the conservative ministers were not committed to extreme measures of hostility. He enjoyed preaching most in places thoroughly committed to the movement. When appointments were made in such places great assemblies gathered from a wide extent of country. Meetings of this character were held at Basking Ridge, New Jersey, the home of John Cross, which Whitefield had not visited before, and at other New Jersey

---

[1] *Ibid.*, p. 65; *New England Weekly Journal*, January 27, 1741.

[2] Webster, *op. cit.*, p. 390.   [3] *Christian History* for 1744, p. 391.

[4] Beadle, *The Old and the New*, pp. 85–87.

[5] Whitefield, *Journal*, No. 7, p. 78.

towns, at Fagg's Manor, Pennsylvania, where there was a general weeping, and at Nottingham, where the people stood in the rain to hear him. There were precious times at Bohemia, Maryland, the home of Hutchinson and the Bayard family, friends of the evangelical cause.

We have seen how, early in the year, in one of those picturesque out-of-doors meetings, where thousands of hearers had yielded assent to a message which awakened every holy aspiration, Presbyterian oppositon lifted its hoarse voice of protest.   Now in the autumn it opened a campaign of pamphlets against Whitefield.   When he reached New York upon leaving New England there came to his notice a "bitter pamphlet," called the *Querists*, printed with the approval of the presbytery of New Castle.   The tract began in a tone of moderation, but it ended by doubting the genuineness of the conversion of great numbers because they had never before shown any regard for religion, and by charging the chief instrument in their reclamation with being a Papist under the disguise of a Calvinist.   Whitefield immediately published a letter in New York in answer to the tract.[1]   The *Querists* presents the argument of the conservatives against Whitefield personally and against the movement of which he was the chief promoter.   The answer is a luminous illustration of the spirit in which Whitefield met criticism, however hostile, that had a semblance of sincerity.

One class of objections was from the point of view of men trained in the exact terminology of the Shorter Catechism against one who employed scriptural figures and the broad expressions of Pietists and mystics. The authors of the *Querists*, for example, objected to his speaking of Christ being spiritually formed in men's hearts, as being equivalent to the Quaker Barclay's representation of the "Christ within."[2]   Charles Tennent urged in defense of Whitefield that his expressions were capable of an orthodox interpretation, and that this should be given them, since his teaching in general was in accord with Calvinistic doctrine.[3]   But Whitefield in his answer acknowledged the justice of the criticisms of this class.   He excused himself as insufficiently trained in the Calvinistic system when he left the university, having been led into the light by degrees.   He therefore desired the prayers of his critics that he might be led to a more perfect understanding of the truth, and to this end he professed himself ever willing to receive correction.[4]

[1] Boston *News-Letter*, November 27, December 4, 1740.

[2] *Querists*, p. 23.

[3] *Pennsylvania Gazette*, October 16, 1740.

[4] Whitefield, *A Letter . . . . In Answer to . . . . . Querists*, pp. 59–64.

Another class of objections was directed against this catholic spirit. If a Calvinist could join the Lutherans and Arminians in religious work, would he not turn Papist at Rome? If a churchman reproved clergymen for leaving the Church and at the same time encouraged dissenters in their separation by preaching in their meeting-houses, was he not helping to perpetuate the rent in the robe of Christ?[1] To these objections Whitefield answered that his design was to bring poor souls to Christ. In prosecuting his mission to meet this design he hoped to avoid the extreme of bigotry on the one hand, and on the other that of confounding order and decency.[2]

A third class of objections was bitter and even malignant in statement. Whitefield declined to answer them in detail. His critics charged him with superstition. They insinuated that his aims were sinister. They doubted the reported charitable deeds of the English Methodists. They denounced their associates who idolized a raw, unstable novice with his "unturned cakes," even to the overthrow of Presbyterian judicatories and discipline. They expressed their contempt for the rabble which now deserted its former ministers. They decried convulsions and revelations. Whitefield regretted that they had dipped their pens in gall and suggested that their insinuations were contrary to the charity which the apostle recommends.

It is a relief to turn from the impotent rage of good men whose horizon was appallingly narrow to a splendid exhibition of evangelical catholicity. A permanent monument to the influence of Whitefield in the eventful year of 1740 was erected at Philadelphia. When the English church was denied him in May many of his supporters, in the warmth of their indignation, proposed to build him a great church. He feared that the evangelical revival would be narrowed by the adoption of such a policy to the walls of a building and to the limits of a party.[3] Yet after his departure the plan was accommodated to his principles, as will presently be explained, and in July the trustees announced their purpose to erect a large building.[4] In November, upon his return to the city, he preached sixteen times in the New Building, as it was called, though it was not yet covered.[5]

[1] *Querists*, pp. 40–43.

[2] Whitefield, *A Letter . . . . In Answer to . . . . Querists*, p. 67.

[3] Whitefield, *Journal*, No. 6, p. 40.

[4] *Pennsylvania Magazine*, quoted by Pennypacker, *Origin of the University of Pennsylvania in 1740*, p. 413.

[5] *Pennsylvania Gazette*, November 27, 1740.

The purpose of the New Building was twofold. Whitefield says: "None but orthodox experienced ministers are to preach in it, and such are to have free liberty, of whatever denomination."[1] It was also to be a charity school, and the appointment of its master was committed to Whitefield, who was made one of the trustees. Lest the building should be appropriated to the use of a single denomination, it was provided that one trustee should be a churchman, one a Presbyterian, one a Baptist, one a Moravian, and so on till the number was complete.[2] The New Building lacked the financial backing of a permanent organization, and it was built for an itinerant preacher who could only after long intervals occupy its pulpit. Yet it was a memorial to the charm in the name of Whitefield. It will be necessary in its proper connection to say something more concerning the Old Academy, as it was afterward called, and the generous fulfilment of its twofold trust. The picture of Whitefield preaching to a delighted multitude in the roofless New Building, even in the cold days of November, fittingly closes the story of a wonderful year in the Middle Colonies.

[1] *Pennsylvania Gazette*, December 4, 1740.

[2] Franklin, *op. cit.*, p. 149.

CHAPTER VI

THE SCHISM IN THE PRESBYTERIAN CHURCH IN THE YEAR 1741

At the beginning of the year 1741 the two great itinerant evangelists, George Whitefield and Gilbert Tennent, were beyond the borders of the Middle Colonies. Yet the conservative Presbyterian ministers looked in vain for a subsidence of the religious excitement. The Great Awakening had now become a people's movement.

The Old Side ministers lost a splendid opportunity to build up their churches and contribute to a moral revolution. They desired both these things, but they lacked vision. All recognized that there had been religious decay. Now was the time to arrest it when the people were awake. When the need of the hour was warmth of appeal to men to live for higher things, they were warm only in their denunciation of their associates who were making such appeals. The answer of Whitefield to the *Querists* had been so conciliatory that the authors might well have declared themselves satisfied. He had made every doctrinal concession to them that they could demand.[1] Yet they returned to the attack upon him in their former bitter spirit.[2] They opposed impressions and impulses. So did Jonathan Edwards, but he entered into hearty co-operation with Whitefield.[3] They opposed bodily agitations. So did Jonathan Dickinson, but he was none the less a promoter of the revival.[4] The relations of Whitefield and the Boston pastors were beautifully harmonious, but in that city these bodily agitations were openly discouraged and were absent from his meetings.[5] Indeed the preaching of Whitefield, notwithstanding its overmastering appeal to the emotions, was not of a character to terrify and so result in cries and faintings as was the preaching of Jonathan Edwards and Gilbert Tennent. These phenomena

---

[1] *South Carolina Gazette,* January 22, 1741.

[2] *Pennsylvania Gazette,* June 11, 1741; August 26, 1742.

[3] Dwight, *Edwards,* p. 147. Yet Edwards did not oppose bodily agitations.

[4] *Christian History* for 1743, p. 155. Gilbert Tennent denies that he was an instrument of promoting bodily agitations, but claims that from their first appearance in New Jersey he spoke against them (*Examiner Examined,* p. 46). Neither Blair nor Rowland desired to produce them.

[5] *Christian History* for 1744, p. 386.

were therefore most unusual in his ministry and never were regarded as having any relation to true conversion. The conservatives opposed convulsions. So did Whitefield himself. He looked upon them as blemishes, the work of Satan to cast discredit upon the revival.[1] The Old Side ministers did not avail themselves of the assistance of the great orator. They did not adopt any of the measures which were open to them to promote a revival. They stiffly closed their pulpits to the possessors of evangelistic gifts, or so grudgingly opened them that their hostility was apparent.[2] Thus they appeared to the zealous of their own congregations and to pastors who threw themselves unreservedly into the movement as enemies of the work of God, even as strangers to a work of grace in their own hearts.

The storm center was the presbytery of Donegal.[3] This, as we have seen, was the frontier region of Pennsylvania. Its territory lay on both sides of the Susquehanna River. The crisis came over the question of intrusion, the preaching of one minister in the parish bounds of another without his consent. It is often assumed that Gilbert Tennent and his associates intruded upon other pastors, but their denial is supported by the weight of evidence.[4] Whitefield, to be sure, had no hesitation to preach within the parishes of clergymen who denied him their pulpits. He asserted his right as a gospel minister to preach anywhere.[5] Without resort to intrusion and field preaching the Methodist Revival in England would have been an impossibility, at least as a movement within the national church. Gilbert Tennent did not hold quite the same theory. He held that it was a time of great opportunity, when religious necessity took precedence of ecclesiastical regulations,[6] at least of relatively unimportant administrative measures and usages proper enough to a time of normal church activity. Therefore he was free to preach in vacancies under the care of other presbyteries than his own, even before the law

---

[1] Gledstone, *George Whitefield*, pp. 226, 227. Whitefield's *Journals* report frequent melting times in his audiences, but it was seldom that demonstration was carried farther. Gilbert Tennent, while discouraging extreme appearances, thought them otherwise to be explained than as coming from the devil. Gilbert Tennent, *Examiner Examined*, p. 46.

[2] *Christian History* for 1744, p. 260; Tracy, *The Great Awakening*, p. 350.

[3] Webster, *A History of the Presbyterian Church*, p. 160.

[4] Hodge, *Constitutional History of the Presbyterian Church*, Part II, p. 140.

[5] Whitefield, *Journal*, No. 4, p. 18; No. 5, p. 36; No. 6, p. 11.

[6] *New England Weekly Journal*, January 27, 1741. This principle, to which he made frequent appeal, was clearly stated in the Directory. *Confessions of Faith*, p. 179.

prohibiting this was repealed by the synod. He was not incapable of intruding upon pastors unfraternal enough to deny him their pulpits, but that he did so there is no proof. It is to be remembered, however, that he did not recognize the binding authority of the law just mentioned, but he fully recognized the legal power of a pastor within the bounds of his own parish. In fact he repudiated the charge of intrusion upon the fields of other pastors.

The theory and practice of the New Brunswick party were further illustrated by the course of Samuel Blair, who was the pioneer of the party in the territory distinctively Scotch-Irish. He went before Tennent and Whitefield to Nottingham as an itinerant evangelist. He preached in other places in the presbytery of Donegal.[1] It is evident that he had not intruded upon pastors before the meeting of the synod in 1740, for he then threatened in the name of the evangelical ministers to answer the invitations of people whose pastors opposed the revival by going to preach to them.[2] At a meeting of the presbytery of Donegal in that same year a representation was made that he had intruded upon several of the members.[3] Notwithstanding the vague charges then made, it can be shown that he did not intrude but went upon consent reluctantly given. The nature of these so-called intrusions is described in his own account of the revival in the province. According to this account ministers whose discourses were searching and whose manner was pathetic were earnestly sought by vacant congregations; and ministers who did not put their shoulders to help yielded to the importunities of their people to invite such brethren to their pulpits.[4] Robert Smith, son-in-law of Blair, writing afterward in defense of the New Side ministers, says: "Some of our ministers preached at their brethren's invitation in their pulpits; but that they ran into their congregations with a design to rend and divide them is not true."[5]

Not all advocates of revivalism kept within the law of their church by threatening to apply the higher law of necessity. Samuel Blair was a visitor from the neighboring presbytery of New Castle, but all the ministerial members of Donegal were hostile to the revival, with two exceptions, Alexander Creaghead, of Middle Octorara, and David Alexander, of Pequea. These two men were independent sympathizers with the New Brunswick party. Creaghead co-operated with this party

---

[1] Whitefield, *Journal*, No. 6, p. 43.

[2] Hodge, *op. cit.*, Part II, p. 135.   [3] *Ibid.*, p. 141.

[4] *Christian History* for 1744, p. 260.

[5] Smith, *The Detection Detected*, p. 120.

until August, 1741, but in principles he was a Cameronian.   Notwithstanding his strict notions on subscription Creaghead held that ministers
ought not to be confined to particular charges.   He roamed about as
the most impassioned advocate of the revival.   He preached within the
territorial limits of the congregation of Francis Alison, of New London,
in the presbytery of New Castle, without the consent of the pastor.
Alison complained to the presbytery of Donegal, and that body, meeting
at Middle Octorara, suspended Creaghead from the ministry.[1]

Like Creaghead in his insurgency was his friend David Alexander, the
young pastor at Pequea.   He also for a little time co-operated with the
New Brunwsick men.   He intruded upon the field of Samuel Black, of
the Forks of the Brandywine.   Black was not a man of unsullied reputa-
tion, as is evidenced by his suspension for a season by the presbytery.
Alexander gloried in preaching in the congregational bounds of such a
minister.   The presbytery met at Alexander's meeting-house in May,
1741, and he too was suspended from the ministry.[2]   The fact that these
two cases of intrusion were tried by a presbytery, and appeal was carried
to the synod, indicates that there was no clear basis for similar action
against the more prominent promoters of the revival.   This world
movement generally put the loyalty to the church universal above the
loyalty to the denomination.   For this reason the Cameronians and
even the Seceders of Scotland raved in impotent fury against Whitefield.
But here we find men of the narrow Cameronian type uniting with Whitefield and his supporters.   Creaghead and Alexander were evidently not
esteemed by Blair and Smith as actually identified with their party.
Creaghead particularly was an extremist not only in his Cameronianism
but in his utter disregard of presbyterial authority and in the divisive
methods which he employed.[3]   In that day of extravagant asseveration,
when the licensing of one, two, or three men each year was denounced
as the letting loose of a horde of illiterate licentiates, so too the unregulated activities of two men easily led to an outcry against all revivalists
as rebels against ecclesiastical authority and as intruders everywhere
upon the parishes of their brethren.

Thus the battle-ground between the extreme advocates of the revival
and extreme conservatives was in the presbytery most remote from New
Brunswick.   This was due to several causes.   The majority of the
Donegal ministers were rigid Presbyterians, placing stress on subscrip-

[1] Hodge, *op. cit.*, Part II, p. 142.

[2] *Ibid.*, pp. 143, 144; Webster, *op. cit.*, pp. 162, 438.

[3] *Ibid.*, p. 435; Gilbert Tennent, *Examiner Examined*, p. 121.

tion to formulas and on presbyterial authority. Yet inconsistently they resisted compliance with the rule of the synod requiring examination of candidates for the ministry upon their gracious experiences, and they were culpably lenient in their treatment of grave moral offenses.[1]

Another cause of intense partisanship was in the character of the people. Scattered among the immigrants were those who clung defiantly to Cameronia i principles. Others sympathized as hotly with the Seceders of Scotland. The Scotch and Scotch-Irish in their numerous revivals have been peculiarly susceptible to unrestrained emotionalism, with its attendant phenomena.[2] At the same time the rigid formalists were hostile to the cultivation of the subjective side of religion. Extremes therefore met not only among the ministers of the presbytery but among the people. Feeling ran high on account of the trials of Creaghead and Alexander. The supporters of the revival in several of the churches presided over by ministers bitterly antagonistic to it petitioned the presbytery of New Brunswick at the close of May to send supplies to them.[3] Some of these people were probably bent on their erection as separate congregations.

The synod met at Philadelphia on May 27, 1741. Gilbert Tennent had just returned from New England. He was still under the spell of his phenomenal success and was as determined and aggressive as ever. The New Brunswick men were confident that the seal of divine approval was upon the course which they had so earnestly pursued. The first question that came up was the right of the two suspended members to seats in the synod. Objection was made especially to Creaghead, and the contest was waged over his case. Charges and counter-charges were made by the Donegal presbytery and Alison on the one side and by Creaghead and his congregation on the other.[4] Gilbert Tennent thought that in a great crisis the saving of life was more important than the precise observance of mere rules of procedure, but he was not prepared to maintain that Creaghead had correctly applied the theory. Neither was he willing to desert Creaghead and admit the intrusion without justification. His hoped-for solution, it seems, was in the mediating findings of an investigating committee, censuring both Creaghead for his lawless support of a good cause and Alison for his

[1] Gillespie, *A Letter to the . . . . Presbytery of New York*, p. 7; Webster, *op. cit.*, p. 457.

[2] Davenport, *Primitive Traits in Religious Revivals*, pp. 60, 87.

[3] MS Minutes of the New Brunswick Presbytery for June 2, 1741.

[4] *Records of the Presbyterian Church*, pp. 154, 155.

opposition to the revival.   After three days' debate the synod could not yet agree upon the personnel of the committee which was to go to Middle Octorara for the trial of Creaghead.   In the heat of debate it was easy to pass from the actual case before the synod to the larger question of the attitude toward the revival itself.[1]

A temporary adjournment was the moment of quiet before an explosion.   Robert Cross, junior pastor of the church at Philadelphia, brought in a protestation, signed by several members, which he read in the presence of the congregation that filled the galleries.   Indignant that the presbytery of New Brunwsick had violated the act of the synod upon examination of candidates, they declared that they themselves would recognize no determination of the synod which was contrary to their own judgment.   They pronounced the members of the offending presbytery and those who upheld them in their practices to have forfeited their right to sit in the synod.   They asserted that they, the protesters, and those who should join them were the true Presbyterian Church, while the persons now accused in this protest were alone to be looked upon as guilty of schism.   The only privileges remaining to the accused, hereby denied the right to vote or to defend themselves, were confession of guilt and satisfactory assurance of future obedience.   Thus the champions of order, protesting loudly their loyalty to it, committed an act of supreme disorder.[2]

The New Brunswick men were not disposed to be excluded without a word of defense, but it was impossible for them to be heard in the uproar.   The moderator left his chair.   There was a rush of elders to sign the protestation.   It was a disorderly marshaling of forces, each party, the New Side and the Old Side, thinking itself in the majority. The sympathies of the galleries were vociferously with the members protested against.   When it was found that the New Sides were in slight minority, they and a large part of the congregation left the meeting-house. Thus without a formal vote and without the semblance of a trial the men who had a year before protested against an act which they regarded as exceeding the power of the synod were now excluded from membership in it.[3]

The disruption of 1741 was quite as appalling a fact to the men of that generation as the division nearly a century later was to the membership of the reunited Presbyterian Church which had become opulent,

---

[1] Gilbert Tennent, *Examiner Examined*, pp. 89, 121, 126; Hodge, *op. cit.*, Part II, p. 147.

[2] *Records of the Presbyterian Church*, pp. 155–58.

[3] Hodge, *op. cit.*, Part II, pp. 147–61.

influential, and continental in its jurisdiction. How lamentable was this first division of forces, with all the resultant alienation and dissipation of energy at a time when the back country of the Middle and Southern Colonies was filling up with a population overwhelmingly Calvinistic, prevailingly Scotch-Irish, and therefore as virile as it was turbulent! How unfortunate that the Presbyterian synod did not catch the new enthusiasm of the day and press forward to the work of education and unification! But better strife and division than stagnation and death. The sequel will show that the minority, thrown out of the synod because too zealous to be altogether decorous, leaped forward to do the work which the synod had rejected and, with an energy born of the Great Awakening, magnificently succeeded.

While the disruption had such momentous meaning to the infant church and to all observers keenly interested in religious developments, the actual number of ministers engaged in the struggle was ridiculously small. The voting of lay elders may be disregarded, as they generally followed their pastors. The whole ministerial membership of the synod was less than fifty. All were required to attend the meetings of the synod, but the distance was so great for members living farthest from Philadelphia that frequently the large New York presbytery was not represented at all. This was the case in 1741, while there were absences from all the presbyteries except Donegal, which was that year exercised over the cases of Creaghead and Alexander. Accordingly there were but twenty-six ministers present, and nine of these were from Donegal. Of these twenty-six members twelve were protesters, including seven of the Donegal ministers, and nine were protested against, including the two remaining Donegal ministers, so that the decision really fell to five men. Of these five moderates two were sympathizers with the revival, who in spite of their conservative misgivings threw in their lot with the protested against, and three were critics of the revival, who in spite of their disgust at the unparliamentary procedure of the protesters either took their stand with them or bolted for home. At any rate, in the disorderly counting of supporters the conservatives were successful, and the advocates of revivalism withdrew.[1]

On June 2, the day following the disruption, the presbytery of New Brunswick held a meeting at Philadelphia. It was attended not only by its own members but by other ministers now excluded or withdrawing from the synod. The first minute declared that the exclusion was without just ground. An appeal to the public in answer to the protestation

[1] *Ibid.*, p. 167; *Records of the Presbyterian Church*, pp. 155–58.

was decreed.   Undaunted, they resolved to form themselves into two presbyteries.   The excluded members at first took their expulsion to be a finality.   They assumed the state of an independent Presbyterian Church.   But soon, upon reconsideration, they contended that they were still legally members of the synod of Philadelphia and entitled to seats in it.   Then their own temporary supreme judicatory was called the meeting of the conjunct-presbyteries.[1]

The protestation had charged the accused members with holding principles "diametrically opposite" to the doctrines of the church.[2] The New Brunwsick men, resenting the reflection upon their orthodoxy, formally declared that they adhered as closely and fully to the Westminster Confession as did ever the synod of Philadelphia in any of its public acts concerning it.[3]   The protestation had further charged the presbytery of New Brunswick with having dissented from the Presbyterian system of church government, divesting the judicatories of all authority.   At their first meeting after the schism the excluded ministers declared their unanimous adherence to the Directory.   But these deliverances on doctrine and government must be interpreted in harmony with the New Side principle that the church does not possess legislative power. One of the unpublished sermons of Gilbert Tennent is quite as emphatic on this question as anything that was ever uttered by Jonathan Dickinson.[4]

Having determined matters of organization and declared themselves on doctrine and government, the reformers were ready to concert measures for the extension of the revival and the establishment of congregations devoted to the cultivation of experimental religion.   At this meeting in June petitions were received from a great number of congregations and parts of congregations that were favorable to the revival. The greater number were vacancies, most numerous in the district assigned to the presbytery of Donegal, but some were as far distant as the James River in Virginia.   Several congregations, already served temporarily by New Side men, applied for appointments, but it is significant that at this early date a number of congregations under the charge of Old Side ministers, members of the Donegal presbytery, besought the New Brunswick presbytery to send them preachers.   At Nottingham Gilbert Tennent had advised his hearers to seek such minis-

---

[1] MS Minutes of the New Brunswick Presbytery for June 2, 1741.

[2] *Records of the Presbyterian Church*, p. 157.

[3] MS Minutes of the New Brunswick Presbytery for June 2, 1741.

[4] Gilbert Tennent, MS of sermon on James 4:12.

trations as were helpful to them.   Now they were acting upon his advice, forgetful, however, of the limitation which he had set.

In addition to these petitions for supplies it was expected that provision would be made for preaching in the New Building, where undoubtedly this meeting of the presbytery was held.   The purpose of the great house was to provide an undenominational preaching-place for Whitefield and other promoters of the revival.   Whitefield had commended Tennent and his associates, and they had been the most active in preaching there, though it cannot be supposed that before the schism there was an organized congregation.   Most of those who flocked to the New Building whenever there was an opportunity to enjoy the new ministry of life and feeling had been converted under the preaching of Whitefield, and all denominations were represented among them.[1] A number of these supporters of ardent evangelism who were Presbyterian in sentiment now permanently withdrew from the First Church, and they were joined by a larger number of others in forming a separate congregation.   At this meeting of the presbytery Finley, Treat, and Rowland were appointed as the first supplies of the new congregation.[2]   At the same time, in congregational meeting, Gilbert Tennent baptized eight Quakers.[3]   Therefore the organization of this Presbyterian congregation, which soon became and long remained the most influential in the Presbyterian communion, may be dated Wednesday, June 3, 1741.

In answer to the supplications from vacancies and dissatisfied congregations or parts of congregations appointments were made for itinerating journeys by New Side evangelists.   The meetings were to be held on both Sundays and week days.   These evangelists were James Campbell, John Rowland, William Tennent, Jr., Richard Treat, David Alexander, and Samuel Finley.

James Campbell, the probationer who in 1739 had stopped preaching for a season because of the conviction that he was unconverted, was directed to make a circuit of sixteen congregations, mostly within the bounds of the presbytery of Donegal.   He was sent as far west as the frontier town of Carlisle and as far east as Greenwich in Cohansey, New Jersey.[4]

[1] MS Records of the Second Presbyterian Church for May, 1743, and September 25, 1746.

[2] MS Minutes of the New Brunswick Presbytery for June 3, 1741.

[3] *Pennsylvania Gazette*, June 11, 1741.

[4] Whitefield, *Journal*, No. 5, p. 42.

John Rowland was directed to follow Campbell. This is the first notice of the longer itinerations of this remarkably awakening preacher. Wherever he went there were outbursts of feeling, and strong men were broken down under the new consciousness of sin. From this time until the removal of his residence from Maidenhead to Charlestown, Pennsylvania, he was occupied with these evangelistic journeys. It was when thus engaged that his message met with a surprising reception at New Providence. In the space of two months the awakened were led through the various stages of conviction and conversion—a shorter period than had generally been required at Maidenhead. At the neighboring settlement of Charlestown the people made profession of various denominational beliefs, but all was in vain in the opinion of Rowland. He saw only vileness in their lives. Here too he met with success, though not so marked as at New Providence. As the result of a great ingathering the united churches of Charlestown and New Providence called Rowland to become their pastor. He died at Charlestown in 1745, universally esteemed. Like so many other New Side evangelists, he died in the morning of life, and, like theirs, it was a morning of strange brilliancy. Long after in the region of Norriton and Providence grandparents told their grandchildren of the wonderful days of Rowland.[1]

The tour covering the widest extent of country was assigned to Samuel Finley, probationer. He was to begin at Nottingham in the Donegal presbytery, where he had served before the rupture, to pass through Baltimore county in Maryland, then, having preached at Dover and Lewes in Delaware, to cross to Cape May in New Jersey, and, completing his great circuit, to preach at Greenwich in Cohansey, the final appointment of Campbell. This was the beginning of Finley's successes in South Jersey.[2] He had been preceded in this destitute region by Samuel Blair, Gilbert Tennent, and Whitefield.

The protestation had operated to release the energy of these splendidly gifted young zealots who with the afflatus of prophets and the martyr spirit of apostles made the journeys outlined for them. The Old Sides, by excluding so violently and irregularly the young and vigorous preachers of the New Brunswick party, but increased their own difficulties. The number of separations was far greater than is

[1] Rowland, *A Narrative of the Revival . . . . in . . . . Hopewell, Amwell, and Maidenhead . . . . and New Providence;* Alexander, *Log College,* pp. 245, 246; Murphy, *The Presbytery of the Log College,* pp. 107, 108, 202-4; Gilbert Tennent, *A Funeral Sermon,* p. 39.

[2] Brown, *History of the Presbyterian Churches in West or South Jersey,* p. 19.

indicated by the supplications first made to the presbytery of New Brunswick. There were divisions in nearly all the congregations in the four Old Side presbyteries.[1] The best of men were blinded, not so much by their own zeal as by the extravagant language which had been used against them. According to the protestation the doctrines of the New Side men were heretical, their government anarchical, and their revival spurious. Therefore the young evangelists broke in upon the congregations of ministers who had developed such hostility to spiritual religion, confident that they were delivering sheep from wolves and from hireling shepherds.[2] While we may assert with some degree of confidence that the preachers who were permanently and genuinely New Side men had never before the disruption of the church intruded upon their brethren, now they went wherever the cry of the discontented called them. The conservatives were not behind them in resort to intrusion, for the Old Side presbyteries sent supplies to the congregations in their bounds whose New Side pastors had been excluded by the synod.[3] They treated the excluded ministers as heretics and schismatics now barred from their communion. They attacked them in the press with a virulence which had not been reached before in their most objectionable contributions.[4] The New Side men, though always charged with censoriousness, were, in print at least, as sober and dignified as their opposers were violent. The synod thus lost all influence with these stirring evangelists. Yet it was not they that caused the divisions. It was a spontaneous uprising among the people. It was an outburst of religious feeling against the coldness of the age.

[1] Webster, *op. cit.*, pp. 185, 197.

[2] Boston *News-Letter*, September 23, 1742.

[3] Webster, *op. cit.*, pp. 408, 446, 461.

[4] *Pennsylvania Gazette*, November 5, 1741; August 26, October 21, December 8, 1742; Boston *Evening Post*, April 2, 1744.

CHAPTER VII

PERIOD OF EXPANSION AND ORGANIZATION

The period extending from the close of the year 1741 to the time when Whitefield was again itinerating through the Middle Colonies in the years 1745–46 was a period of expansion and organization. It was then that the operations of the Moravians attracted universal attention. The Second Presbyterian Church of Philadelphia became the center of New Side influence. The synod of New York was organized. New Side missions were founded, which were to exercise a profound influence on world-wide missions. Schools upon the model of the Log College were established. Most remarkable of all was the extension of the revival to Virginia. Thus the awakened religious life did not confine its expression to evangelistic endeavor, strictly construed, but found new channels for its pent-up powers in related activities of an ever-widening range.

1. *Zinzendorf's Pennsylvania synods.*—What Whitefield was to the English-speaking colonists Zinzendorf was to the German. And as the former fraternized with Presbyterians, Baptists, Quakers, and Moravians, so the latter in 1741 resigned his office of bishop of the Moravian Church that he might not confine his testimony to one denomination.[1]

When, therefore, Zinzendorf landed at New York late in 1741 and began a systematic visitation of the German settlements in Pennsylvania, interest in the Moravians, keen already because of their connection with the religious awakening in Germany and England and their missionary successes in South Africa, was heightened by the visit to the Middle Colonies of the gifted but visionary nobleman who stood at their head.[2] Coming in the spirit of Whitefield, Zinzendorf very naturally desired to take full advantage of his connection with the Methodist leaders, but he claimed too much when he announced that his brother, George Whitefield, was a son of their church, brought to the blood of Jesus by Peter Boehler.[3]

[1] Sachse, *German Sectarians*, p. 460.

[2] Boston *News-Letter*, September 25, 1740; *New England Weekly Journal*, November 4, 1740; *Pennsylvania Gazette*, February 24, 1743.

[3] *South Carolina Gazette*, August 30, 1742.

The student of the Great Awakening finds striking illustrations of the syncretic tendencies of the Moravians of that period. One of their missionaries in the province of New York testified in court that he had not separated from the Church of England by joining the Moravian brotherhood, for the Moravians were united with all Protestants.[1] Just so Zinzendorf was a Lutheran minister and a Moravian minister at the same time. The Moravians at Bethlehem endeavored to conciliate the Siebentagers of Ephrata by observing both Saturday and Sunday as days of rest.[2] As Zinzendorf found a bewildering confusion of religious beliefs among the Germans he desired to unite the evangelistic efforts of the various sects.[3] Therefore he sought to form "one congregation of God in the Spirit," though its members were to retain their denominational affiliations. To this end a synod was called to meet at Germantown on January 12, 1742. There came to it Lutherans, German Reformed, Mennonites, Schwenkfelders, Dunkers, Siebentagers, Separatists, one hermit, and Moravians.[4] Seven of these synods were held. Though the purpose was worthy of all praise, Zinzendorf failed to make the distinction between ecclesiastical acts, like baptism and ordination, which were proper to denominational organizations alone, and those common endeavors which could be undertaken without violating the distinctive beliefs of the various bodies represented. The result was that after the third meeting four of the denominations withdrew from the movement. The spirit of contention, quieted for a season, broke out again.[5]

The result of the mission of Zinzendorf was thus a disappointment to him. Nevertheless it was highly beneficial to the religious interests of the Germans. Many of the Separatists in Pennsylvania, religious enthusiasts without denominational organization, when called from their isolation by Zinzendorf, joined the Moravian brotherhood, adding strength to that body of earnest evangelists and missionaries.[6] Conversions under the preaching of the count and his co-workers were numerous. After he had served the Lutheran Church at Philadelphia for the greater part of a year a separation took place,[7] and the Moravians

---

[1] *Ecclesiastical Records of the State of New York*, pp. 2851–54.

[2] Sachse, *German Sectarians*, p. 440.   [3] *Ibid.*, p. 442.

[4] Brumbaugh, *A History of the German Baptist Brethren*, p. 474.

[5] *Ibid.*, p. 484.   [6] Sachse, *op. cit.*, p. 423.

[7] This was occasioned by the arrival in 1742 of Henry Melchior Muhlenberg as a missionary sent from Halle, Germany. Spangenberg, *Life of Count Zinzendorf*, p. 298; Bolles, *Pennsylvania Province and State*, II, 378.

of the congregation organized according to the Herrnhut pattern.[1]
Indeed both the Lutheran and German Reformed authorities in Europe
were stimulated by the labors of Zinzendorf in America to send superintendents and pastors to their destitute coreligionists.[2]   Even the Dunkers
found the suggestion of their annual meetings in the synods of Zinzendorf.[3]   Thus on the one hand the tendency to excessive individualism
among the Germans was checked, and on the other aggressive church
extension was undertaken through emulation of Moravian aggressive-
ness.

Successful as were the Moravian itinerants among the Germans and
measurably even among the English-speaking people, their master
passion here as in other lands was the prosecution of missions among the
heathen.   The story is a long chapter of heroic efforts, cruelly obstructed,
particularly at the very first, in the province of New York.   Christian
Rauch had opened his mission at Schecomoco in Dutchess county,
New York, in 1740, and great was his triumph to be able to present three
converts at the second of Zinzendorf's synods.[4]   But Horsmanden, of
the New York council, defended the provincial law which was enacted
against the missionaries as vagrant preachers and popish emissaries on
the ground that they were suspected of endeavoring to seduce the Indians
from their fidelity to His Majesty, and that they, like all the German
Sectarians and the Quakers, refused to take the oath to the government.[5]
The report of the sheriff and the examination of the missionaries before
the council, however, amply refuted the charges of wrong-doing.[6]   Yet
the missionaries were ordered to desist from further teaching and to
leave the province.[7]   Fortunately the province of Pennsylvania was
still liberal, and so was Connecticut in this respect.   In these colonies
the Moravians continued their missionary activity when for a time New
York was closed by a wall of bigotry.

2. *Calvinistic recoil from Moravian catholicity.*—Whitefield had
described Gilbert Tennent as one of the most catholic men he knew, but
Tennent's catholicity was not broad enough to include the Moravians.
Zinzendorf, on his journey from New York to Philadelphia, was invited
to a conference at New Brunswick.   The oracular, paradoxical, mystical
language of the count was exasperating enough to one of Tennent's

[1] Ritter, *History of the Moravian Church in Philadelphia*, p. 19.

[2] Kuhns, *The German and Swiss Settlements of Colonial Pennsylvania*, pp. 164, 165.

[3] Brumbaugh, *op. cit.*, p. 477.

[4] Sachse, *op. cit.*, p. 466.   [6] *Ibid.*, p. 2851.

[5] *Eccl. Rec. of New York*, p. 2906.   [7] *Ibid.*, p. 2861.

training. The mental processes of the two men were so different, and both were men of such determination, that neither could appreciate the truth for which the other stood or realize their essential unity. Based upon the statements of the count at New Brunswick, an unfavorable estimate of the Moravians was drawn up and published in book form. This was followed by another.[1] Zinzendorf answered through the newspapers, and Tennent continued the debate through the same medium.[2]

Calvinistic criticism of the mystic philosophy of the leader was aroused to this public protest by the methods of evangelism adopted by the brotherhood and the directions given to religious seekers. The Moravians made use of lay itinerants who traveled through the country with smiling faces and affable manners, warmly expressing sympathy with all Christians but drawing converts to their own communion.[3] These methods, in the opinion of Gilbert Tennent, were divisive and dangerous. He was too much of a Presbyterian to tolerate lay preaching and was quite as insistent upon an educated ministry as were his Old Side antagonists. The Moravians made little use of the law in dealing with the unconverted. They did not consider the prolonged distresses attending law-work necessary. In this, strangely enough, they were at one with the Old Side Presbyterians. The brotherhood defined faith as persuasion, and in this agreed with the Scotch Seceders. The Moravians believed in perfection, as did the Quakers. Therefore the Moravians were described by the Calvinistic supporters of the revival as Antinomian, Arminian, and Quakerish in principle. It was intimated that their removal from Romanism was slight.[4]

Contact with a strange people who had been among the most active promoters of the revival in the country of its origin, yet whose doctrines were so foreign to his own, and whose methods threatened to divide his own following, persuaded Gilbert Tennent, erroneously, as a student of this world movement must conclude, that his proper affiliation was with the men of his own race and doctrinal training, from whom he had

[1] Gilbert Tennent, *Some Account of the Principles of the Moravians*, and sermon on Rev. 3:3.

[2] *Pennsylvania Gazette*, May 19, June 30, July 7, 1743. The account of Zinzendorf was contributed by Boehler, who remained in America after the departure of the count.

[3] Gilbert Tennent in a sermon published with *Some Account of the Principles of the Moravians*, pp. 52, 54, 65, 66; Livingston in *Independence Reflector*, January 4, 1753.

[4] Gilbert Tennent, *op. cit.*, p. 61.

lately separated.   Early in 1742 he wrote his letter of lamentation over
the schism in the Presbyterian Church to Jonathan Dickinson, the most
eminent supporter of the revival still in the membership of the synod of
Philadelphia.   The letter has been called a recantation.   For months
Tennent had been in an agony of spiritual desertion.   He regretted
his mismanagement of the debate in the synod; he felt a disposition to
fall on his knees and beg both parties to be at peace.   After his collision
with the Moravians he was apprehensive of the danger in divisive measures as practiced by them.   The news from New England also disquieted
him.   The extravagances of his friend Davenport had subjected the
revival to ridicule.   Tennent in his letter of lamentation gives a list of
these objectionable practices, but the only one properly censurable was
Davenport's unfortunate habit of pronouncing by name individual
ministers unconverted.[1]

David Evans, Old Side Presbyterian, asserted in print that wherein
Tennent condemned Davenport he passed sentence upon himself.   Evans
suggested that the letter of Tennent carried "ill designs under a new
mask."[2]   A New England opposer arrayed "Gilbert against Tennent,"
making charges similar to those of Evans.   The publication of Tennent's
lament inspired him to explain that it was the manner of performing
what he still considered a duty that he regretted as mismanagement.[3]
The storm of criticism reawakened his combative spirit, but he soon
returned to his plea for harmony.   He pursued his new aim with the
same whole-hearted determination which he had previously given to the
spread of the revival.

That the essential cleavage in colonial society on the question of
religion did not follow the lines of race and inherited creed but was
determined by individual attitude to the new evangel was demonstrated
by an exciting occurrence in the spring of 1742.   This was the famous
trial of William Tennent, Jr., in April, at Trenton, before the malignant
chief justice of New Jersey.   It seems almost incredible that a minister
who inspired all who knew him intimately, among them the Hon. Elias
Boudinot, his biographer, with veneration as for a man of extraordinary
saintliness should be subjected to the indignity of standing trial on the
charge of perjury.   The more incredible would it be, if one were unacquainted with other examples of partisan hostility in colonial days, that
this trial was in effect a retrial of John Rowland on the charge of horse

[1] Boston *News-Letter*, July 22, 1742.

[2] *Pennsylvania Gazette*, August 26, 1742.

[3] Boston *News-Letter*, September 23, 1742.

stealing—the very Rowland who had led the reformation at the neighboring town of Maidenhead and who was then faming through the adjoining province in a blaze of glory. The evidence clearly proved the innocence of Rowland and the truth of the alibi which Tennent had furnished him, yet the acquittal appeared to the saint of Freehold, whose whole life was filled with what he judged to be divine interpositions, as nothing less than miraculous.[1] Gilbert Tennent charged the opposers of the revival with joining the profane in the persecution of Rowland and greatly exulted in the thoroughness of the vindication of both his brother and his friend.[2] Even this experience did not quench his new passion for Presbyterian Church unity.

3. *The Second Presbyterian Church of Philadelphia.*—Though Gilbert Tennent, the very soul of his party, was exerting all his powers of masterful leadership to reconcile the contending factions within the synod of Philadelphia, for the New Brunswick men claimed still to be members, he evidently recognized that it was quite impossible to drive the demonstrative admirers of Whitefield, who had put themselves as a congregation under the charge of the presbytery of New Brunswick, into the chilling atmosphere of the old First Church. Such a course would have been disadvantageous both to revivalism and to Presbyterianism, for the new congregation was speedily to become the leading church of the denomination and one of the greatest in the country. Philadelphia was and is the capital city of American Presbyterianism. The old First Church, though originally congregational in polity and not actually the oldest Presbyterian church in the Middle Colonies, nevertheless gave its name to the first presbytery and the first synod and is appropriately regarded as the mother church of the denomination. What the First Church was to the Old Side Presbyterians the Second Church was to the New Side. "No church ever had more distinguished ruling elders from the old times down to its later days."[3] It was a power in the political and social life not only of the city but of the province and country.[4] The names of its Hodges, Bayards, Boudinots, Hazards, Eastburns, Redmonds, Bourns, Shippens, and Grants were widely known in the eighteenth century, and many of them in the nineteenth as well.

[1] Green, "The Trial of the Rev. William Tennent," *Princeton Review*, July, 1868; Alexander, *Log College*, pp. 127–34.

[2] Gilbert Tennent, *Examiner Examined*, p. 127.

[3] Nevin, *History of the Presbytery of Philadelphia*, p. 300.

[4] Beadle, *The Old and the New*, p. 43.

The historian of this venerable church dates its organization as a Presbyterian society in the year 1743, when Gilbert Tennent became its pastor,[1] but in reality its distinct existence as a congregation began, as already shown, in June, 1741. The minutes of the presbytery for the next two years show that in answer to repeated supplications nearly all the great lights of the party were sent as supplies, some of them as stated supplies.[2] Finally, in May, 1743, a call to Gilbert Tennent was brought into the presbytery. In August commissioners presented their arguments, those from New Brunswick for his continuance there, and those from Philadelphia for his removal to that field of greater influence. He himself desired the dissolution of his former pastoral relation, and the presbytery acceded to his request in view of the difficult situation at Philadelphia.[3]

How these transactions were regarded by the Old Side opposers of the revival is reported by the witty but unscrupulous Fleet, of the Boston *Evening Post*. In their view Gilbert Tennent had gone to a congregation of Separatists, using the term in the opprobrious sense of an irregular and unrecognized organization. Furthermore, this congregation had taken possession of the "great Babel," built for Whitefield, though the Moravians claimed the better right to it. A running fire of criticism on Tennent, supplied by Old Side enemies in Philadelphia, was maintained by this newspaper. They soon noted a change in the pastor himself. Tennent, it was said, had "cast off his native clumsiness," and from a "slouch" had become a "beau" with a "polite and courtly air."[4] It is quite true that he now yielded to the taste of polite society not only in dress but in the delivery of his sermons. His usual method in the time of his itinerations, when as a forceful preacher he was unsurpassed, was that of extempore speaking. In Philadelphia he became so wedded to his notes that in his later years he negatived the choice of a colleague by his congregation because the people were so immoderately desirous of extempore preaching. The candidate thus opposed was George Duffield, almost, if not quite, as powerful a preacher as Tennent had been in his prime. Evidently the people of this congregation, active, emotional, and demonstrative, retained Whitefield's aversion to reading as a method of pulpit delivery.[5]

---

[1] Beadle, *The Old and the New*, p. 11.

[2] MS Records of the New Brunswick Presbytery for May 29 and August 2, 1742; MS Records of the Second Presbyterian Church for July 7, 1742.

[3] MS Records of the New Brunswick Presbytery.

[4] Boston *Evening Post*, November 14, December 12, 1743; January 16, April 2, 1744.

[5] Gilbert Tennent, MS on Use of Notes, 1762; Alexander, *Log College*, pp. 58, 59.

Thus from the multitude of Whitefield's converts and supporters a goodly company of the most ardent had put themselves as a distinct congregation under the presbytery of New Brunswick. A constantly growing membership proved that Whitefield's spirit was in the new leader and his workers, but a surprise came to this congregation after it had been eight years in possession of the great house of worship. On January 25, 1749, the report was made at a congregational meeting by the trustees of the New Building that "agreeable to their deed of trust" they had decided to convey the title to the trustees of the public academy "in trust for the uses and purposes in their original deed expressed." One of the conditions of the transfer was that Mr. Tennent and his congregation were to have free use of the New Building as a place of worship for three years. This concession to the peculiar relation existing between this people and their hero, Whitefield, must have seemed to them less than the equity of the case demanded, yet they could make no protest, for it was one of the original articles of agreement that this great brick monument to New Light evangelism was not to be devoted to the exclusive use of any one denomination.[1]

This unforeseen difficulty stirred a man of Gilbert Tennent's metal to determined effort to erect a monument to New Side Presbyterianism surpassing in beauty and churchly dignity the great auditorium of which he was soon to be dispossessed.[2] But many of his people, warm advocates of emotional religion though they were, were Methodists and Quakers in their hostility to ornament and churchliness in religious architecture, just as they favored plainness of dress and speech. Tennent would call his meeting-house a church and suit the building to the name, braving the ridicule of Anglicans without and the disgust of Methodists within. Furthermore, their New Light energy had not yet brought them large wealth. Franklin, who was a trustee of the projected academy and also of the New Building, suggested that the pastor appeal to the citizens generally for subscriptions.[3] This Tennent did, throwing his unconquerable will into the work. The result was that the gifts of outsiders far exceeded the contributions of the members.[4] Nearly all the officers of the province, county, and city subscribed to this public enterprise. The liberal-minded of all denominations contributed.[5] It was, however, to the ministers of his own party that Tennent looked for

[1] MS Records of the Second Presbyterian Church.

[2] Gilbert Tennent, *Divine Government*, pp. 51–53, 66–68.

[3] Franklin, *Autobiography*, pp. 156, 157.

[4] Gilbert Tennent, MS Remonstrance of 1762, p. 19.

[5] MS of Subscription List; Gilbert Tennent, *Divine Government*, p. 55.

the aid that should give success. Subscriptions were taken, accordingly, at Neshaminy, Maidenhead, Abington, White Clay Creek, and Fagg's Manor. With what elevation of spirit the pastor opened the new house in June, 1752, with two sermons! He saw a divine providence in all the train of surprising events that began with the formation of this society. There was providence too in the donations of large-souled gentlemen who were above every suggestion of bigotry and blind party spirit. Though the Christian world was divided into parties which too often censured the conduct of their brethren, there was really one visible Kingdom of Christ with many branches. Every true Christian, there-fore, should rejoice in the success of every society that retained the fundamental principles. Tennent in conclusion summarized the law and gospel in humility, charity, and kindly feeling.[1]

4. *The New Side synod of New York.*—The narrative of the early formative years of the foremost New Side congregation has taken us in time beyond the organization of another body which had even greater significance in the ultimate triumph of New Side principles. The synod of New York was formed in 1745, but the efforts in the preceding years to avoid the necessity of its organization must first be recounted.

In the year 1742, before the meeting of the synod of Philadelphia, George Gillespie, supporter of the revival but stickler for order and regularity, published a letter addressed to the presbytery of New York. He appealed to the members of that presbytery to be present at the coming meeting at Philadelphia. The conjunct-presbyteries were to meet at the same time and place. His contention was that the illegal protest ought to be dropped and all members "allowed to meet together judicially." He defined a protest as an appeal of a minority from the action of the majority to God's bar, but the protestation of 1741 was the condemnation of the minority by the majority without a trial. He traced the beginning of the division to the "antiscriptural, lording act" of 1738 requiring synodical examination of candidates.[2]

The synod of Philadelphia met in May, 1742. A greater number of ministers from the New York presbytery attended the meeting than had ever come before. The protesters claimed that they and those who had acted with them were the synod of 1741. They refused to be called to account by absent members or by any judicatory on earth. Six of the seven ministers present from the New York presbytery, one Old Side minister, and several elders joined in a protest against the illegal

[1] Gilbert Tennent, *Divine Government*, pp. 1, 6, 45, 51–56, 66–69.

[2] Gillespie, *A Letter to the . . . . Presbytery of New York*, pp. 3, 15, 18, 22.

exclusion of the year before and against the refusal of the protesters of the previous year to have the legality of their protest determined by the present synod. They declared that the members excluded by protest, in violation of scriptural rule and Presbyterian usage, were still members of the synod. Finally they made solemn declaration against all the pamphlets published in these parts which reflected on the work of divine grace which had been carried on so wonderfully in many congregations.[1]

These efforts in 1742 were futile, and the rent was the wider in 1743. The real obstacle to reconciliation was the spirit of division in the local churches which was sweeping over them like a whirlwind. All the New Side ministers could not have stayed it, had they joined in Gilbert Tennent's lament. As it advanced, the Old Side ministers became more embittered, and their public attacks were the more abusive.[2] Then Gilbert Tennent replied that when ministers conspired to blacken the revival and brand it with terms of contempt he did not see how God-fearing church members could sit under their ministrations.[3] Therefore the possibility of reconciliation was more remote in 1743 and 1744 than it was before.

In May, 1745, three commissioners came as representatives of the presbytery of New York. They requested the consent of the old synod for the erection of a new one—the two bodies to act in mutual concert and brotherly kindness. The synod replied that the withdrawal of the New York brethren was without just ground, yet they would maintain charitable affections toward them.[4]

On September 19, 1745, the synod of New York was organized at Elizabethtown, New Jersey. Nine ministers of the presbytery of New York were present, nine from the presbytery of New Brunswick, and four from the New Side presbytery of New Castle. A testimony to the work of God's glorious grace carried on in these parts of the land was unanimously adopted by the synod. The fundamental articles of synodical union are of special significance as attempting a solution of questions upon which the radical and moderate supporters of the revival had not been in entire agreement.[5]

---

[1] *Records of the Presbyterian Church*, pp. 159–62.

[2] Boston *Evening Post*, July 26, November 1, 1742; January 10, 1743; *Pennsylvania Gazette*, August 26, October 21, 1742; December 8, 1743; Boston *News-Letter*, October 28, 1742.

[3] *Pennsylvania Gazette*, August 26, 1742.

[4] *Records of the Presbyterian Church*, pp. 175–79.

[5] *Ibid.*, pp. 232–34.

The first article reaffirmed the adopting act of 1729, by which the Westminster Confession was accepted as an excellent statement of the Calvinistic system, without binding the candidates for the ministry to agreement with the verbal statement of any single article of the confession. That act denied the legislative power of the synod and made the Scriptures the supreme law of the church. Thus the New Side synod was established on the basis of progressive orthodoxy.[1] This was in accordance with the spirit of the whole evangelical revival, whether in Germany, Great Britain, or America, to put the emphasis on life, conduct, and experience, to throw off the shackles of formal statements of belief adopted in past time, and to make possible the restatement of doctrines with more ample recognition of principles brought to the fore by this world-wide quickening.[2]

By the second article a solution of the problem of final authority in matters of discipline was attempted. This had been a weak point in the argument of Jonathan Dickinson in 1722 and of Gilbert Tennent in 1739. They had both sought a constitutional limitation by which the individual and the minority were to be protected from the tyranny of the majority. In 1722 Dickinson restricted ecclesiastical censures to cases of heresy and scandal.[3] In 1739 Tennent in the name of the presbytery of New Brunswick refused to obey two acts of the synod regarded as illegal and tyrannical. Now it was decided that when a member could not in conscience abide by a determination of the majority and, the synod was not able to make concession to his scruples, judging the determination essential to the well-being of the churches, the dissenting member promised peaceably to withdraw from the synod. Distinction was thus made between the circumstantial and the essential. Gilbert Tennent always maintained that the rules of the synod, violated by the New Brunswick men, were upon circumstantial matters.[4]

The two remaining articles promised the avoidance of divisive methods, no condemnation of ministers by other means than those pre-

[1] Briggs, *American Presbyterianism*, pp. 269–72; Gillett, *History of the Presbyterian Church*, I, 88–90.

[2] Jonathan Edwards was the philosopher and theologian of the Great Awakening. Bellamy and Hopkins were his successors, uniting Calvinism with the pietistic and humanitarian spirit.

[3] Dickinson, *Sermon Preached at the Opening of the Synod*, p. 21.

[4] Gilbert Tennent, *Irenicum*, p. 99. Among the Tennent manuscripts is a carefully prepared sermon for a presbyterial meeting on Christ as the only lawmaker. Its date is about 1753, but the same theory appears in the writings of Tennent, Blair, and Gillespie before 1745. The contest between the presbytery and synod was on government, not on doctrine, but the same principle applies to both.

scribed in the Directory, no granting of supplies outside of presbyterial bounds to parties separating from Presbyterian and Congregational churches, and the maintenance of correspondence with the synod of Philadelphia.[1] There was no re-enactment of the rule requiring synodical examination of candidates, regarded by all supporters of the Log College as illegal. On the contrary, there was a distinct agreement that all possessing a competent degree of ministerial knowledge, orthodox in doctrine, regular in life, diligent to promote vital godliness, and willing to submit to the discipline, were to be cheerfully admitted to this union. Several ministers, trained at the Log College, who would have been barred from membership in the old synod by its law enacted in hostility to that school, were constituent members of the new synod, and others were to be admitted, until death claimed in 1746 the incomparable teacher of zealous evangelists.

5. *Missions to the heathen.*—The new fire would have flashed like powder and gone out but for organizations such as have been described. They gathered the converts, maintained the new ideals, and sent out men of splendid enthusiasm to extend the Great Awakening among peoples and in regions not reached before. The new birth of religion throughout the world resulted in the establishment of modern missions. Accordingly in America missions to the heathen were undertaken as a direct result of the Great Awakening. A glance will be given to the efforts in behalf of the negro and then a more extended account of the missions to the Indian, which form an important stage in the development of modern missions.

Although the first German immigrants to Pennsylvania, straight from the home of Pietism, spoke out against slavery, the first powerful champion of the black man was Whitefield. He addressed words of special tenderness to the negroes. A new appreciation of a common humanity came to whites and blacks as they wept together. Though efforts were made in different colonies in behalf of the negroes, some directly inspired by Whitefield[2] and others stimulated by his appeal,[3] the stupendous

[1] There was such granting of supplies from 1741 to 1745 both by the New Brunswick and the Old Side Presbyterians.

[2] Boston *News-Letter*, August 21, 1740; *New England Weekly Journal*, May 6, 20, June 3, 1740; *Pennsylvania Gazette*, November 27, 1740; *American Weekly Mercury*, January 8, 1741; New York *Weekly Journal*, February 4, 1741; *South Carolina Gazette*, March 6, 1742.

[3] A year after Whitefield's letter advocating the Christian training of slaves his friend Hugh Bryan published a letter denouncing the clergy of the establishment for their failure to show pity to the perishing. A year later he and his brother were

task of their evangelization was left to the Methodists and Baptists of a later day. It was necessary that the Great Awakening in successive advances should win the allegiance of a dominant portion of the white population of the states where slaves abounded before the Christianization of the negroes, the greatest missionary triumph of the eighteenth and nineteenth centuries, could be effected.

Missionary effort in behalf of the American Indians, also powerfully stimulated by the Great Awakening, was rewarded by earlier fruitage than were Whitefield's enterprises for the uplift of black men. Indeed, in the period before the revival the New England governments had co-operated with Scotch and Scotch-Irish societies in the maintenance of missions to the Indians in their borders. The results were not commensurate with the efforts put forth.[1] But when the revival swept over New England the Indians were caught in the same movement.[2] These successes gave new life to missionary endeavor. The mission at Stockbridge, Massachusetts, conducted by Jonathan Edwards after his dismissal from Northampton, came into direct contact with the Indians of New York, and its beneficial influence was felt far into the interior of that province.[3] Dartmouth College, founded by Eleazer Wheelock, was another gathering-point of Indian youth from the Middle Colonies. Samson Occum, Wheelock's first Indian pupil, and a number of other missionaries who looked to Wheelock for direction and support operated in the Middle Colonies. Whitefield's influence in England brought very considerable aid to these Indian missions conducted by friends of the revival.[4]

---

indicted for holding religious meetings for negroes. In the meantime, but more than a year and a half after Whitefield's letter was issued, letters of the bishop of London were advertised exhorting masters to instruct their negroes in the Christian faith. Dissenting pastors, supporters of the revival, seem to have been the first to take public action in adopting the proposals of the bishop. Finally Garden published an Account of the Negro School at Charleston for the year 1743. *South Carolina Gazette*, January 8, September 5, 1741; March 27, April 17, 1742; April 2, 1744. Ramsay refers to a report of the school published in 1752. Ramsay, *South Carolina*, II, 467.

[1] *New England Weekly Journal*, December 13, 1733; September 9, 1735; October 26, 1736; Dwight, *Edwards*, p. 449; Robe, *Christian Monthly History*, No. 5, pp. 3–12.

[2] Boston *Weekly Post-Boy*, October 5, 1745; Prince, *Christian History* for 1744, pp. 21, 109, 113, 154.

[3] Dwight, *op. cit.*, p. 534.

[4] Wheelock, *A plain and faithful Narrative* and *A Continuation of the Narrative;* Brainerd, *The Life of John Brainerd*, p. 347.

These New Light enthusiasts did not come to an absolutely untilled field, for the English Society for the Propagation of the Gospel had been and was still co-operating with the province of New York in missionary endeavor among the Indians. The society sometimes employed Dutch pastors. The purposes, however, were less religious than political, for they were conceived as counter-movements against the French and Jesuits.[1] Mention has been made of a genuinely religious effort among the Indians of New York, that of the Moravians. They were remarkably successful, because the missionaries threw all their powers with passionate self-sacrifice into the lowly service of their heathen brothers. They brought them a religion of fervor and taught them the common arts of civilized life.[2] The expulsion of the Moravians, however, was compensated, in part at least, by the coming of men of kindred spirit.

Far more important than these New England missions in the Middle Colonies were the missions conducted by the New Side Presbyterians. Heroic as were the efforts of the Moravians in the province of Pennsylvania, these Presbyterian missions had a wider influence in stimulating missionary interest among the English-speaking people. The New Side Presbyterians joined with the Scotch Society for Propagating Christian Knowledge in the establishment of Indian missions in the Middle Colonies. Asariah Horton began his labor on Long Island in August, 1741. James Davenport had already begun a remarkable work among the Indians there. The missionary came, therefore, at the most opportune time. His earnestness overcame the native lethargy of his hearers. Though they were not convulsed by bodily agitations, like so many of their white neighbors among whom Davenport preached, they went through the usual deep distresses, ending in voiceful exultation, which were regarded by the New Side Presbyterians as the normal method of conversion. The converts often spoke of seeing Christ, but Horton explained the expression as due to their figurative speech. The Indians meant that they saw Christ by the heart, for the New Side Presbyterians had great horror of raptures, visions, and all pretense to immediate revelation.[3] Horton continued his mission up to the year 1753. Webster, the historian, reported one hundred years afterward that two of the Indian churches still remained.[4]

Though Horton earned honorable mention, the name that is spelled in capital letters is that of Brainerd. There is no more saintly figure

---

[1] *Eccl. Rec. of New York*, pp. 1443, 1466.   [2] Brainerd, *op. cit.*, p. 73.

[3] Robe, *op. cit.*, No. 5, pp. 14–66; No. 6, pp. 1–17.

[4] Webster, *A History of the Presbyterian Church*, p. 465.

in American missionary annals than that of David Brainerd. A historian of missions has said of Brainerd's work in New Jersey that "at Crossweeksung his success was perhaps without a parallel in heathen missions since the days of the apostles."[1] His diary is a classic and came as a personal call to a number of gifted young men who later were recognized as among the greatest missionaries to non-Christian lands.[2] He was another appointee of the correspondents of the Scotch Society.

David Brainerd stood at the head of his class at Yale and was in his third year there when Gilbert Tennent's preaching was rewarded by the conversion of a large number of the students. The college authorities showed little sympathy with the movement. The rector fined some of the students who followed Tennent to Milford. Brainerd was heartily devoted to the revival and in private conversation spoke harshly of one of the tutors. For this he was expelled from college.[3] After Brainerd's appointment as a missionary he was sent in April, 1743, to Kaunaumeek, New York, and later to the Forks of the Delaware, where now at Easton a church bears his name. In September he returned to New Haven, hoping to take his degree. He made the most ample apology. There was no question of his attainments in scholarship, but in spite of the entreaties of Aaron Burr and Jonathan Edwards the college authorities held out stiffly and unreasonably for an additional year's residence. The rebuff given Brainerd, following numerous acts of hostility to the revival, was so resented by the ministers of the New York presbytery, who were nearly all graduates of Yale, that some of them attributed the founding of Princeton College to this incident as the main cause.[4] In June, 1744, Brainerd was ordained by the presbytery of New York in violation of the rule of the synod, from which the presbytery had not yet formally withdrawn.[5] The synod in a letter to Rector Clap condemns the presbytery for "improving in the ministry" scholars that Clap had expelled.[6]

Brainerd's missionary journeys were in the provinces of New Jersey and Pennsylvania as far west as the Susquehanna River. From March to November of one year he traveled three thousand miles. In June, 1745, he began his mission at Crossweeksung, New Jersey, bringing together at that point a number of the scattered bands of Indians. The

---

[1] Brainerd, *op. cit.*, quoting Ashbel Green, p. 80.

[2] Notably Henry Martyn, of India and Persia.

[3] Edwards, *Brainerd*, p. 50.

[4] Alexander, *op. cit.*, p. 78; Stearns, *Historical Discourse*, p. 176; Brainerd, *op. cit.*, p. 56.

[5] Edwards, *Brainerd*, p. 142.   [6] *Records of the Presbyterian Church*, p. 186.

successive revivals here were the marvel of that time and have been with succeeding generations of readers. His converts were proposed by neighboring pastors to their congregations as examples of piety. The meetings were frequented by the members of white congregations, who saw in the experiences of the children of the forests experiences in every respect similar to their own in the revival which had previously been so remarkable among the whites. There were the same results in the lives of the converts, the mastery over drink, and the new religious energy transmuted into industrial energy. Brainerd gathered his Indians together on Indian lands at Cranbury, and the progress of their village astonished all visitors.[1]

David Brainerd made his last visit to the Susquehanna when already stricken with disease; afterward by slow stages he journeyed back to New England, where he died in the home of Jonathan Edwards. John Brainerd, his brother, succeeded him in the mission. His were the discouragements attendant upon the training of such a people. The greatest difficulty was not in the refractory nature of the Indians but in the rapacity of Chief Justice Morris and his fellow conspirators, who ejected not only the Indians from their new town of Bethel but large numbers of white farmers from their holdings.[2] The Indian town of Brotherton was then founded with ample legal protection.[3] A generation after the death of John Brainerd the remnant of the Indians migrated to western New York, where they amalgamated with the Oneidas.[4]

6. *The revivalists as educators.*—The new impulse given to education by the evangelical revival was even more significant than the new enthusiasm for missionary endeavor. The Great Awakening as a popular movement and as a return to primitive Christianity appeared to its opposers to be unfavorable to education. The Separates of New England, the Baptists, with whom to a considerable extent they united, the Moravians, and after them the Methodists, all made use of lay preachers and advanced to the regular ministry men who did not possess college diplomas. Yet the Separates founded the Shepherd's Tent at New London, and the other bodies have an honorable history as promoters of education. But whatever the attitude of these bodies, which were then looked upon as irregular, the leading Calvinistic revivalists were everywhere insistent upon ministerial education and favorable to popular education. They held this position and struggled to found schools at

---

[1] Edwards, *Brainerd*, pp. 194–307; Brainerd, *op. cit.*, pp. 79–81, 113.

[2] *Ibid*, pp. 153–58, 284–91.

[3] *Ibid.*, pp. 292–97.   [4] *Ibid.*, pp. 417–23.

the very time during which they were ridiculed in public print as the apostles of ignorance.[1]

The founding in 1726 of William Tennent's school has been described in an earlier chapter. For twenty years this school of the prophets justified the name of Log College. He sent out as many young men into the ministry in the last five years of his life as he had in the preceding fifteen. This was itself a fruit of the quickened religious interest. In 1742 he was so bowed down by the weight of years that he begged assistance from the presbytery, and supplies were granted him. In 1743 Charles Beatty, trained by him, was ordained as his colleague.[2] Beatty was later widely known for his journeys among the Indians, his service as chaplain to provincial troops, and his voyages to foreign parts in the interest of Princeton College and church extension. He had not the quiet, scholarly tastes to continue the Log College. Therefore when the patriarch of education died in 1746 the Log College ceased to exist.[3]

The great majority of the young men trained at the Log College entered upon their work after the schism of 1741. They were sharply distinguished from the men trained in European universities, as most of the Old Side ministers had been. The distinguishing marks are well indicated by the criticisms of George Gillespie upon the latter,[4] though he was himself educated in Scotland, and by the newspaper attacks of unnamed correspondents upon the former. The Old Side ministers had been destined by their parents to the ministry without being able to tell of a spiritual crisis in their lives and without a burning zeal to make converts to Christ. They resented any prying into their secret experiences, though this was required by the order of the synod and the discipline of the church. The Log College men, on the other hand, were caught up by a wave of revivalism. They dared not prepare for the ministry until they had passed through a period of conviction, had attained assurance, and believed themselves driven into the ministry by divine compulsion. Most of these young men followed other occupations, from which they turned to ministerial preparation. At the completion of their studies they went out like the apostles to turn the world upside down. Then their enemies cried out, "Could the great Gilbert be persuaded to remit these strollers to their looms, their lasts,

[1] Boston *Evening Post*, April 2, October 15, 1744; Boston *Gazette*, July 24, 1744; *Pennsylvania Journal*, June 30, 1743; *South Carolina Gazette*, July 4, 1743.

[2] MS Minutes of the New Brunswick Presbytery for December 14, 1743.

[3] Alexander, *op. cit.*, p. 247; Murphy, *Presbytery of the Log College*, p. 68.

[4] Gillespie, *op. cit.*, pp. 5, 6, 20.

their packs, their grubbing hoes, from whence in his great zeal he took them, to support his father's Log House College, we might soon hope to see a new face of affairs; but this is not to be expected."[1] All the sixteen or eighteen New Side ministers who were trained at the Log College were men of fiery zeal, and fully half of them were preachers of extraordinary power. Such were the two Blairs and Samuel Finley, who were equally eminent as educators; and such were the four Tennent brothers, John Rowland, William Robinson, Charles Beatty, and John Roan.

Samuel Blair, one of the strongest of this group of strong men, established a classical and theological school at Fagg's Manor upon the model of the Log College. His first pupil, Samuel Davies, was ready for licensure in 1746.[2] The expenses of this promising student were borne by William Robinson. The reward of both instructor and benefactor was that as a preacher Davies was the admiration of England and America, and as president of Princeton College he was greatly beloved. Yet Davies declared that in all his travels he heard no preacher equal to his teacher, Samuel Blair.[3] Other students at Fagg's Manor were Dr. John Rodgers, of New York, Alexander Cumming, of Boston, James Finley, brother of Samuel, and Robert Smith, of Pequea, all leaders of note. After the death of Samuel Blair in 1751 his school was continued by his brother, John Blair, also educated at the Log College, until his election in 1767 to a professorship at Princeton.[4]

Another famous educator trained at the Log College and ranking with Samuel and John Blair was Samuel Finley. There was no more aggressive itinerant than he. After his settlement at Nottingham, Pennsylvania, he established an academy there which attracted not only

[1] Boston *Evening Post*, April 2, 1744.

[2] Blair is said to have opened his school soon after his removal to Fagg's Manor, but Davies may have come under his instruction at Shrewsbury, New Jersey, for Davies received the rudiments of classical training under Rev. Abel Morgan, Baptist pastor at Middletown, New Jersey. Webster, *op. cit.*, p. 549; Murphy, *op. cit.*, p. 88. The famous John Rodgers entered Blair's school in 1743, completed there his academical studies, including the moral and physical sciences, as well as the languages, and made considerable progress in the study of theology. "At Mr. Blair's Academy, Mr. Rodgers was so happy as to find a number of young gentlemen, of excellent talents, and of eminent piety, preparing for the gospel ministry, in whose friendship he found much comfort, and whose society contributed not a little to his improvement."—Miller, *Memoirs of Rev. John Rodgers, D.D.*, pp. 17-23.

[3] Alexander, *op. cit.*, p. 193; Webster, *op. cit.*, pp. 430, 550.

[4] Alexander, *op. cit.*, pp. 197, 198; Murphy, *op. cit.*, pp. 87-95.

students preparing for the ministry but others as well.   Among the distinguished men educated at Nottingham were Governors Martin, of North Carolina, and Henry, of Maryland, Dr. Benjamin Rush, of Philadelphia, and Dr. William M. Tennent, of Abington, son of Charles Tennent and grandson of the founder of the Log College.   Upon the death in 1761 of Samuel Davies, president of Princeton, Samuel Finley was elected his successor.   He held the office till his death in 1766.[1]   It was during his presidency that an amazing revival swept through the college, when about half the entire number of students were converted, so that nearly the whole college was experimentally Christian.[2]

The relation of the Log College to Princeton is intimate but not so direct as its relation to private schools giving collegiate instruction at Fagg's Manor, Nottingham, and Pequea.[3]   Jonathan Dickinson and Aaron Burr, the first and second presidents of the College of New Jersey, as Princeton was called in the eighteenth century, were members of the presbytery of New York and were not Log College men.   Yet the new school was chartered not six months after the death of William Tennent, and its ideals were the same as those of the Log College.   The ministers of that presbytery had come to distrust the colleges of New England, much as did Whitefield, his friend Governor Belcher, Jonathan Edwards, and Gilbert Tennent.   In the refounding of the college in 1748 New Brunswick men were prominent, and it was removed eight years later to Princeton, within the bounds of the presbytery of New Brunswick, and centrally located, like Neshaminy, between New York and Philadelphia.   Burr was followed in the presidency by his father-in-law, Jonathan Edwards, whose death soon followed.   His successors in office were Samuel Davies and Samuel Finley.   All these men were great preachers and eminent promoters of the revival.   Their deaths came in rapid succession.   The names of so many presidents who had been foremost in the Great Awakening have indissolubly associated the infancy

[1] *Ibid.*, pp. 95–101; Alexander, *op. cit.*, pp. 204–14; Webster, *op. cit.*, p. 490.

[2] Gilbert Tennent, *Discourses on . . . . Important Subjects*, Preface, pp. iii–x; Davies, *Little Children invited to Jesus Christ*, pp. 13, 14.

[3] This was a school of the third generation from the Log College, for it was established by Robert Smith, who studied under Samuel Blair, who studied under William Tennent, Sr.   At Pequea, McMillan, pioneer of western Pennsylvania and founder of Jefferson College, was educated, as well as other trainers of preachers.   Among them were the two sons of Robert Smith—S. S. Smith, president of Hampton-Sidney and later of Princeton, and J. B. Smith, president of Hampton-Sidney and later of Union College.   Webster, *op. cit.*, pp. 612, 614.

of Princeton University with warm evangelical religion. It was virtually an offspring of the school on the Neshaminy.[1]

Though New Jersey rejoiced in the possession of a college, the provincial government felt no financial responsibility for its maintenance. Therefore the New Side Presbyterians resorted to various expedients to secure funds. Finally in 1753 the synod appointed Gilbert Tennent and Samuel Davies to go to Great Britain to solicit aid.[2] The characteristic perseverance of the one and the affable persuasiveness of the other made their mission an entire success, even though the Presbyterians of England were rapidly approaching Unitarianism and were quite out of sympathy with the evangelical spirit of the visiting Americans.[3] Furthermore, the Old Sides threw obstacles in their way,[4] yet President Finley says that Tennent's mission, in spite of numberless discouragements, was successful beyond all expectation.[5]

The debt of education in the United States to the Great Awakening is merely suggested, not adequately expressed, by the enumeration of the colleges which were the direct fruits of the revival. Among them must be named not only Princeton of the Presbyterians, Dartmouth of the Congregationalists, Brown of the Baptists, Rutgers of the Reformed, but also, as Governor Pennypacker has shown, the University of Pennsylvania, which may trace its pedigree back to George Whitefield as its original founder. The undenominational character of the institution and the attachment of a charity school were features impressed upon academy, college, and university by the original Whitefield enterprise of 1740.[6]

7. *The extension of the revival to Virginia.*—It is one of the contentions of the present writer that the Great Awakening is not to be regarded only in the terms of that extraordinary emotionalism which accompanied impassioned evangelistic endeavor but which was limited in every community to a year or two at the very longest. Moral reform and philanthropic endeavor were essential parts of it, and so were the organic activities which have been outlined in this chapter and which gave form and direction to American Protestantism. Yet it would be a mistake to suppose that in the period following 1742 the religious quickening

[1] Alexander, *op. cit.*, pp. 76–85.

[2] *Records of the Presbyterian Church*, p. 251; Livingston, *op. cit.*, p. 22.

[3] Alexander, *op. cit.*, pp. 54–57; Webster, *op. cit.*, p. 394.   [4] *Ibid.*, p. 555.

[5] Finley, *The Successful Minister*, p. 20.

[6] Pennypacker, *Origin of the University of Pennsylvania in 1740*, p. 421.

nowhere possessed that which in the height of the revival was its characteristic feature. In 1740 Virginia was not ready to give emotional response to the appeal of Whitefield, but in the years following his first visit forces were silently operating which finally issued in passionate expression. The Log College evangelists were the active promoters of this revival. How their itinerations came to be extended to Virginia must first be told.

In the Middle Colonies themselves during this period the revival was generally described as the "late work of God." There was no longer a general excitement kept alive by numerous instances of conviction, and these followed at intervals by the joyous proclamation of conversion. Yet the lives of great numbers were still determined by the decisions they had made in the time of intense religious interest. Isolated communities were reached long after the general movement had passed. The rapid influx of settlers and the growth of the young made possible here and there the exultant announcement of the return of the revival spirit. But the characteristic work of these years was the organization of churches, the building of meeting-houses, and the supplying of congregations with preachers.

Although the revival sent a considerable number of young men to the various schools to prepare for the ministry, the number of congregations appealing for preachers increased in far greater proportion. Several worthy pastors withdrew to the Middle Colonies from Connecticut, where they had been made uncomfortable by the reign of the reactionaries. Among them were Timothy Allen[1] and James Davenport,[2] now reclaimed from their excesses. The supply from all sources was inadequate. There was but one possible method approximately to meet the religious needs of the scattered settlements. That was through an itinerating ministry. The probationers and young ministers were sent upon extensive tours. All the ministers of the presbytery of New Brunswick, always the center of evangelistic endeavor, were sent upon numerous missions, some of them upon long journeys to the southern provinces.

The mission of one of these men led to unimagined results. William Robinson, who was remarkable for his sweet temper and evangelistic power, was sent in 1743 to the new settlements in Virginia and North Carolina on both sides of the Blue Ridge. In after-years aged men told

---

[1] Webster, *op. cit.*, p. 583.

[2] *Ibid.*, p. 531; MS Minutes of the New Brunswick Presbytery for October 13, 1743; May 21, October 16, 1746.

wonderful stories of what they witnessed in their youth where he preached. Congregations were organized by him in the Presbyterian population that was filling up the back country.[1] An earnest invitation was sent to him to preach upon his return northward at Hanover in the Anglican part of Virginia. Here he was introduced to one of the strangest phases of the whole evangelical movement.

A spontaneous revival had developed in that region. The awakened people had no preacher, for they were dissatisfied with the lives and doctrines of the clergymen of the established church. As they were unaccustomed to extempore prayer, none of them dared attempt it. Whitefield had preached at Williamsburg in 1740, but none of these people had heard him. In 1743 a book of Whitefield's sermons was brought to this group of earnest seekers for deeper spiritual life. Mr. Samuel Morris began to read it in his house to his friends who assembled to hear it. "The concern of some was so passionate and violent that they could not avoid crying out, weeping bitterly." His dwelling-house was soon too small to contain the people; thereupon it was determined to build a meeting-house solely for the reading of sermons. Called upon by the court to assign reasons for absenting themselves from church, they took the name of Lutherans, since they knew that Luther was a reformer, and they had little acquaintance with dissenting bodies. Of Robinson's preaching Morris said, "We were overwhelmed with the thought of the unexpected goodness of God in allowing us to hear the gospel in a manner that surpassed our hopes." After the visit of Robinson invitations came to Morris to read sermons in many places, and as a result other meeting-houses were erected and readers appointed.[2]

The newly awakened in Hanover county put themselves under the care of the New Side Presbyterians. John Blair paid them a visit, and later John Roan. The revival was greatly extended by the preaching of these Log College evangelists. Roan was outspoken against the degeneracy of the clergy of the established church. This led to a general alarm, and measures were taken to suppress the movement. Roan was charged with blasphemy, and some of the people who had opened their homes to him were fined. The governor issued an order against any meetings of New Lights and Moravians. The synod of Philadelphia at its next meeting adopted an address to Governor Gooch explaining that these persons against whom charges were made assumed the name of Presbyterians and had been excluded from the synod because of their

[1] Alexander, *op. cit.*, pp. 215–20.

[2] Morris' narrative in Alexander, *Log College*, pp. 221–23.

sending abroad ill-qualified persons to trouble the churches.[1]   The conjunct-presbyteries sent Gilbert Tennent and Samuel Finley to Virginia with an address.   Before their arrival the trial of Morris, which was virtually that of Roan, who had left the province, was held, at which it was proved that the blasphemous expressions attributed to Roan were not uttered by him.   Upon the approach of Tennent and Finley the complaining witness fled, and the governor gave the visiting ministers the liberty to preach.[2]

After the removal of this cloud William Tennent, Jr., and Samuel Blair were sent to the Hanover Presbyterians, making altogether seven Log College men who itinerated in Virginia.   Then Whitefield came, who was readily received by the members of the Church of England. Finally in 1747 Samuel Davies was sent to supply Hanover for a few weeks.   The governor had just issued a proclamation prohibiting all itinerant preaching.   Davies, however, obtained a license to preach in four meeting-houses and later was established as the pastor of the congregations meeting in them.   His ministry was wonderfully successful in the conversion both of gentlemen and, at the other extreme, of slaves.   He was the very soul of urbanity and courtesy, yet the extension of Presbyterianism in the eastern part of the province was effected in the face of official hostility.[3]   Davies assured Commissary Dawson that he had no "ambition to presbyterianize the colony," but he was zealous to "propagate the catholic religion of Jesus in its life and power," since the religious condition of the province was lamentable.[4]

Although we have given our attention almost exclusively to the activities of the Presbyterians during this period of organization, they were by no means the only people who, having caught a new vision, now bestirred themselves to give it concrete embodiment.   The aged Frelinghuysen was gathering about him young men of power to win the Dutch church to revivalistic ideals.   To the aid of the German Lutherans came that superb organizer, Muhlenberg, straight from Halle, the fountainhead of Pietism and the new evangelism.   The Philadelphia Baptist association, strongly Calvinistic and evangelistic, sharing in general the ideals of the New Side Presbyterians, was now advancing to dominant influence in this otherwise unorganized denomination.   But most of these religious bodies were more slow-moving than the militant Ulster

[1] *Records of the Presbyterian Church*, pp. 180–82.

[2] Morris in Alexander, pp. 223–26.

[3] Davies' letter to Bellamy in Alexander, pp. 226–32.

[4] Davies' dedication of the sermon on *Duties*, p. 10.

men, and the story of their activities more naturally belongs to a somewhat later period.

As the leaders of the revival in the days of excited and general feeling had been Presbyterians, with the exception of the chief apostle of the Great Awakening, so now their manifold activities were the most important. We have seen, accordingly, that the New Side Presbyterians were sobered and steadied by the strictures upon their friends, the most radical of the promoters of the revival in New England, and by their own contact with a strange but worthy people whom they could not understand. Then their leaders sought to placate the men of their own blood who had cast them out. Repeatedly rebuffed by the passionate advocates of a passionless religion, the New Side Presbyterians perfected their organization and proved their Presbyterianism by the schools they set up. They cultivated every generous sentiment by admiringly following the fortunes of David Brainerd. Above all they retained their devotion to evangelistic ideals and renewed their old-time fervor by the success of the gospel in the province of Virginia, where the Log College men were the chief itinerant evangelists. Though the account of some of these characteristic activities has been carried to a point beyond the limits of the period to fittingly conclude their story, the account of the triumph of New Side Presbyterianism, as of the triumph of the ideals of the Great Awakening in other denominations, is reserved for a later chapter.

CHAPTER VIII

WHITEFIELD THE PACIFICATOR

While the Great Awakening in the Middle Colonies had passed from the generating to the harnessing of the spiritual energies of the people, Whitefield, who had been the chief instrument of their awakening, was now exemplifying in his own person the characteristic developments of the whole movement. These experiences help to explain the man he was when again he was touring the Middle Colonies in the years 1745 and 1746.

In 1741 Whitefield was back in Great Britain meeting the strangest alternations of fortune. The adoption of Calvinistic principles which had commended him to the active religionists of the colonies was resented by his fellow Methodists of the Church of England, who, in common with a great body of that communion, had practically repudiated its Calvinistic articles. Seward, the wealthy friend of Whitefield, had been murdered by brutal opposers of the revival, and Whitefield was suddenly called upon to meet money advances which Seward had made to him. He was burdened by the orphan-house debts of many thousands with scarcely a penny to pay. Bitterly lamenting his break with John Wesley, deserted by former converts who now stopped their ears lest they should be won by the witchery of his voice to the acceptance of a creed which they detested, and threatened by incarceration in a debtor's cell, the undaunted young warrior, not for a moment questioning the truth of his doctrines or regretting the responsibilities which he had assumed, laid his plans both to pay his debts and to build a great tabernacle on Moorfields in London. He resumed field preaching in the interior with the same striking success in the opening of both hearts and purses which had previously attended it. The Calvinism which was a real, though not insuperable, handicap to the evangelist's mission in England was a compensating advantage when he accepted an invitation to visit Scotland. He had long been a correspondent with the Erskines and felt his heart closely knit with theirs, yet he was unwilling to reject all invitations in Scotland but those of the Seceders and to subordinate his mission as an awakener of spiritual religion to the propagation of fine-spun theories upon church government. The result was that he was rejected by the men who could not monopolize his assistance. One of them, Adam Gib, carried his denunciation of the visitor to such extravagant lengths that in Gib's last days he longed for the power to destroy every copy of his embittered philippic. In spite of the thrusts of reformers and conservatives alike Presbyterian Scotland received the young churchman as a messenger of the King of Glory. Whitefield was formally presented the freedom of cities. Men of all classes owned him their spiritual father. Never since the Reformation had there been such a religious awakening. So great were the gifts of the people to his charities that a foolish cry of impoverishing the country was raised. Back again in England, Whitefield helped the Methodist influence to rise still higher. To his tabernacle, the "soul trap," came not only the multitude but the nobility of the land. Statesmen, men of letters, and actors were there, enthralled by an oratory which they confessed to be without compare. Yet bishops railed against the evangelist as an enthusiast and a fanatic. Church wardens refused to aid the poor who frequented Methodist meetings, and hired ruffians were set upon their preachers. Repeatedly Whitefield was the object of physical violence, and his life was spared as by a miracle. Once a gentleman ruffian, impelled by an instinctive hatred of aggressive religion, made a murderous assault upon the preacher when he was in his bed. Such were the strange vicissitudes of a frail young man who crowded into every week work that would speedily crush the average man. It is not strange that Watts thought him the wonder of the age.[1]

But during these years, and indeed throughout the remainder of his life, Whitefield was never soured by defeat or made vain by victory. Although there was not the least abatement of his zeal, the early note of asperity gave place to ripened sweetness, which won at last the respect and even the affection of early detractors. It was natural that this Methodist reformer at the beginning of his career judged the men who gnashed their teeth at him to be strangers to grace, but he slowly learned the injustice and impolicy of personal recrimination and became tolerant of good men whose prejudices led them astray. It was characteristic too of this movement that at first representatives of all religious schools were brought into practical harmony by the new insistence upon regeneration and piety, but as they put their new earnestness to the exploration of other regions of doctrine and practice it was inevitable that they should divide, as all the world had done before. Thus, though the

[1] Gledstone, *George Whitefield*, pp. 162–224. The colonial newspapers followed his career during all these years but were most interested in his campaign in Scotland.

Methodist societies in the Church of England were divided into two branches, one Calvinistic and the other Arminian, Whitefield was too genial and generous to permit for long a doctrinal difference to separate himself from the Wesleys in the higher unity of Christian love and co-operation. When Whitefield in Scotland, chastened by this separation, suffered abuse from the friends of the Erskines, he still protested his love for them and was betrayed into no bitter words afterward to be regretted. When again he met Ralph Erskine it was to embrace him as a brother. One of the most engaging qualities of Whitefield was his willingness to be the most severe judge of his own conduct, to make the most ample reparation for every possible mistake, to be tolerant of the foibles of good men, to condone the injustice of evil men, and, without counting the cost to himself, to take into his sympathy every man who laid claim to it. In all these things the essential characteristics of the revival attained pre-eminent development in Whitefield.

Such was the man who braved the sea in time of war in response to repeated invitations from the colonies. Whitefield's desire to settle the affairs of the orphan house and audit its accounts constituted another call to America. In the autumn of 1744 he arrived at York, Maine. A number of the ardent supporters of the revival flocked to the port to greet him, but they found him hovering between life and death. When he had partially recovered, his enemies said that his sickness was all a ruse to gain the sympathy of the people.[1] All New England was now sharply divided between the friends and the foes of the revival. The extreme conservatives and the men of rationalistic trend formed a majority of the ruling aristocracy in church and state. On the other side the Boston ministers, the partisans of Jonathan Edwards in western Massachusetts, and a great number of pastors all over New England, with a tremendous popular following, were still warmly devoted to the revival and attached to its chief apostle, Whitefield. The leaders naturally regretted certain popular tendencies of the movement that threatened the overthrow of the ecclesiastical system of New England, though now it may be claimed as one of the glories of the Great Awakening that it set in operation forces which ultimately battered down that system. Whitefield's journey through New England was a tour of pacification. While preaching the same doctrines with the same emotional power, he explicitly warned his hearers from all the extremes which had been revived by the general awakening of religious interest.[2]

[1] Boston *Evening Post*, November 19, 1744.
[2] *Christian History* for 1744, pp. 320, 336.

The same ripening goodness was evidenced in this New England mission which had been noted in Great Britain. It must have been a relief to Whitefield to be free from the danger of physical violence, as he always was in America, but from the day of his arrival at York the reactionary Boston *Evening Post* fulminated against him and, generally withholding the names of the contributors, published vulgar attacks upon him. On the other hand the Boston *Gazette*, as the organ of the evangelicals, defended the cause of reform with dignity and sobriety, while Whitefield himself, when he chose to notice the action of public bodies, answered with convincing sincerity and sweetness. Harvard College had pronounced against him, stung by well-deserved criticism, but Whitefield now and later so persisted in studied acts of good will, notably by his benefactions in the time of Harvard's distress, that at last that institution was compelled to acknowledge his candor and do him honor. The opposers of revivalism sharply criticized the Boston pastors for their immoderate attachment to Whitefield and for their direction of his movements throughout New England, but it was admitted that the evangelist was the idol of the people, so much so that the disturbance of industry threatened an increase of the town rates.[1] Indeed at this time the admirers of Whitefield offered to build for him at Boston the largest auditorium in the country if he would but remain. Though his personal triumph was quite as remarkable now as in 1740, and many were converted in his meetings,[2] no general revival was stimulated by his mission, as when he first visited this section. The ecclesiastical organization of New England and the homogeneity of the population were such that the revival had already run its course in towns where pastors favored the movement. In other towns the only recourse was to the incursions of irregulars, such as the Separates, the Baptists, and later the Methodists. Whitefield did well to strengthen the hand of the evangelical party within the churches of the standing order.

In August, 1746, he passed from eastern Connecticut to Long Island, thus avoiding Yale College, the authorities of which had issued a testimony against him. Having preached in various friendly congregations, he reached New York, where the multitude hung upon his words as in time past.[3] Then, traveling through New Jersey, he was conducted into Philadelphia by fifty horsemen.[4] Though Gilbert Tennent had

[1] Boston *Evening Post*, December 17, 1744.

[2] New York *Post-Boy*, February 18, 1745.

[3] Boston *Gazette*, August 20, 1745; New York *Evening Post*, August 26, September 2, 1745.

[4] New York *Post-Boy*, September 16, 1745.

organized a Presbyterian church which held its stated services in the New Building, the affections of the people went out as undividedly to the great orator as formerly, but in vain did they importune him to make Philadelphia his home and so permanently occupy the building which had been erected especially for him. He made a pilgrimage to Neshaminy to visit the venerable William Tennent, whose hour-glass had almost run out, and then preached his farewell sermon in Philadelphia.[1] Time and excessive labors had not dulled his enthusiasm or deprived his words and gestures of their subtle charm, but friends and enemies remarked that the asperity which formerly marred the pulpit utterances of the young reformer now gave place to a noble charity.[2]

That he so happily blended universal kindness with zeal for righteousness did not result from the stilling of the voices of opposition. In anticipation of Whitefield's visit to New York, Jonathan Arnold again made war upon him in the newspapers, reiterating all his old charges and incorporating a letter of the bishop of Gloucester. The bishop had refused to see the evangelist or to answer his letters. Nevertheless Whitefield had just presented him a volume of his sermons and an account of his orphan house, accompanied by a letter written "in a very obliging manner," but as he continued his itinerating evangelism his ecclesiastical superior thought that his letters deserved no return of civility.[3] As in the case of Arnold's earlier attacks, Whitefield paid not the slightest attention to them now.

Not only in New York but in the Southern Colonies he was driven into the unwilling appearance of undermining the power of his own church when his single aim was to bring men to Christ. His ministrations were more extended in Maryland, where he was importuned to settle,[4] and in Virginia than they had been in his earlier journeys. The Great Awakening as a wave of emotionalism had reached Hanover, Virginia, two years before, and now under the preaching of Whitefield many Church people came under its quickening influence.[5] In Charleston, South Carolina, a hot newspaper dispute was on between the opposers and the promoters of revivalism. Indeed it had been on during all the

---

[1] *Pennsylvania Journal*, September 12, 19, 1745.

[2] *Ibid.*, February 11, 1746.

[3] New York *Post-Boy*, January 21, 1745.

[4] *Pennsylvania Journal*, February 11, 1746.

[5] New York *Post-Boy*, September 16, 23, October 14, November 25, 1745; Morris in Alexander, p. 225.

years of Whitefield's absence, but now it was unusually demonstrative over the validity of Whitefield's suspension from the ministry by Commissary Garden. The brilliant Josiah Smith, of the Congregational church, as defender of Whitefield, was able to show that the English authorities had treated the action of Garden as a nullity, but Garden with learned coarseness would make it appear that either a novice was defended by a knave or a knave by a novice.[1] Yet when Whitefield, bringing with him an atmosphere of serenity, reached the little city of hotbloods, he preached with such winning grace that praises were extorted from some of his worst enemies.[2] Finally he reached his beloved Bethesda, planning when he had settled its affairs to resume his itinerations in the Southern and Middle Colonies.

Whitefield had previously given to the public narratives of his orphan house, Bethesda, with statements of receipts and disbursements. Now his purpose was to join with his business agent in a final statement covering all the operations since the founding of the home. All the accounts and vouchers were laid before the auditors, whose finding was highly creditable to Whitefield's methodical benevolence. Now we find Franklin with evident satisfaction publishing the explanatory letter of Whitefield and a summary financial statement.[3] During the years of the founder's absence the very existence of the orphan house was sometimes questioned, and stories quite as incredible were told about it. The sober accounts of visitors of the highest repute were brushed aside by enemies of the work as fairy tales. Whitefield from the first had hoped to make Bethesda something more than an orphanage. Later he developed his plan to add a college to the orphanage, a plan heartily approved by the Georgia legislature. The home government withheld the granting of the charter and referred the petition of Whitefield and the address of the legislature to the archbishop of Canterbury, who insisted on making the proposed college a Church of England institution. This was a denial of the liberal charter for which the founder petitioned. By the acceptance of a narrow-bottomed charter he would break faith with his contributors, who were largely dissenters. Accordingly the only alternative was the establishment of an academy as an

[1] Not only was disproportionate space given to this dispute for a long time, but frequently extra pages were added to give it room.

[2] *Pennsylvania Journal*, February 11, 1746.

[3] *Pennsylvania Gazette*, May 22, 1746; Franklin, *Autobiography*, p. 131; Gledstone, *op. cit.*, p. 238.

adjunct of the orphanage, with the hope that a more liberal future would permit the realization of his plan.[1]

In the year 1746 Whitefield made his fifth tour through the Middle Colonies. It was more extended and occupied a greater length of time than any previous tour in these provinces, for he arrived in Philadelphia in May and did not preach his final sermon there till late in September. He made excursions into Delaware and Maryland. He traveled in Pennsylvania as far west as Lancaster and as far north as Easton at the Forks of the Delaware. He went to the extremity of New Jersey at Cape May and along the beaten path to New York and Long Island, stopping for the first time at Princeton, which name was beginning to appear on the records of the presbytery of New Brunswick. At the close of his eight days' mission at New York a eulogy in the style of Pemberton was published. It was said that though Whitefield had been preaching incessantly for ten years, and was now but thirty-two years old, he had triumphed over an army of opposers and had demonstrated the correctness of the opinion of Dr. Watts that Providence had raised up the young evangelist to awaken a stupid and ungodly world.[2] After daily preaching in Philadelphia at intervals all summer Whitefield turned southward. Franklin then said of him, "He was never so generally well esteemed by persons of all ranks among us; nor did he ever leave us attended with so many ardent wishes for his happy journey and a safe return to this place."[3] His success in 1746 was quite as remarkable as the burst of applause which first greeted him in 1739, for now the Anglicans, the Old Side Presbyterians, and the Quakers were arrayed against the revival, and his old friends the Moravians were not on good terms with the Lutheran and Presbyterian supporters of the revival. Yet the evangelist now so happily united zeal with charity and the religion of power with Christian courtesy that even violent opposers apologized for the injustice they had done him.[4]

Whitefield journeyed through the Middle Colonies again in 1754, in 1763, and finally in 1770. Enmity skulked in corners, while churches, formerly closed to him, opened their pulpits.[5] Courts would adjourn

---

[1] Whitefield, *Letter to Governor Wright.*

[2] New York *Post-Boy*, August 4, 1746.

[3] *Pennsylvania Gazette*, September 25, 1756.

[4] *Pennsylvania Journal*, February 11, July 3, 1746.

[5] Whitefield preached to a great concourse in Christ Church, Philadelphia, in 1763, and also in St. Paul's, erected by the evangelical party in the Church of England. Watson, *Annals*, I, 385.

and the noise of traffic cease wherever Whitefield was to preach, until the very day of his death. When he was dead America from end to end mourned him as the prophet of triumphant evangelism.[1]

---

[1] Among the many memorial sermons published after his death two demand reference. Ebenezer Pemberton, who had welcomed Whitefield to New York in 1739 and had published such a favorable account of the evangelist that he was promptly invited to New England, now a pastor at Boston, published a funeral eulogy stating substantially what is given above in the text. James Sprout, pastor of the Second Presbyterian Church, Philadelphia, in a funeral sermon affirmed that Whitefield had lived long enough to convince the most malignant of his enemies of his uprightness.

CHAPTER IX

TRIUMPHANT EVANGELISM IN AN AGE OF UNBELIEF

The eighteenth century was an age of unbelief, for the passionless orthodoxy of nominal and apologetic believers was nearly akin to the negations of deists. The world-wide religious awakening was a counter-movement, sometimes threatening to sweep away all opposition but never really changing the trend of the age. The new evangel, however, changed the lives of thousands and called into being a church within the church, a sáving nucleus in almost every communion, composed of divinely illuminated men. They set themselves to square their lives by the new pattern and to win their churches and society to the ideals of experimental religion. It is my immediate task to show how this minority, working against the drift of the age, became a majority in most communions and gave to American Protestantism its dominant characteristics.

The successive journeys of the great Whitefield, outlined in the preceding chapter, won successive generations to a boundless admiration of the man and of the cause of which he was the most conspicuous exponent. Multitudes were converted in his later itinerations, yet never again after 1740 did he set whole colonies afire by his preaching. He contributed, it is true, to movements inaugurated in Virginia by Presbyterians and in the Carolinas by Baptists, which were quite as intense, if not as widely extended, as the revival of 1740. He also prepared the way for the Methodist preachers whom Wesley sent to America. In spite of the diverting of public attention in the Northern Colonies to war and political debate, there were local revivals in New England and more of them in the Middle Colonies, while the South became peculiarly the field of successful evangelism. All these evangelizing efforts of the various denominations and all the related activities were parts of the Great Awakening in its larger and truer meaning. The story of nearly every denomination in the last half of the eighteenth century is that of triumphant evangelism.

1. *Triumphant New Side Presbyterianism.*—When at the beginning of the Revolutionary War and again at the close of the century evangelism was clearly in the ascendancy, the denomination in the Middle

Colonies which counted the greatest number of adherents and most influenced for good other denominations was the Presbyterian. In that denomination by far and away the most influential element was the New Side party. To the day of his death Gilbert Tennent was the leading spirit of that party. We have seen how catholic he was, for he felt quite at home as a worshiper in a Baptist meeting or as toastmaster at a Lutheran banquet. We have seen that hard upon the supreme success of his life he was cast into profound dejection by his share in the Presbyterian schism. It must also be recalled that when the New Side synod was organized in 1745 one of its fundamental agreements aimed at a concert of measures with the Old Side synod for the promotion of common religious interests. At this point I resume the story of the events which led to reunion and demonstrated the superior vitality of the new evangelism.[1]

In 1748 Gilbert Tennent preached a sermon on brotherly love at Philadelphia. In this sermon he warned his hearers from confining their love to men whose opinions coincided with their own upon every minute point and from judging professors of Christianity who were without fervor as being actually graceless. The experienced Christian, he maintained, learns to be merciful from his own blunders and falls. True, there is a temptation to attribute to ill designs the weaknesses and defects of those with whom we differ, but the more Christian course is to hope all things of offending brethren. In fine, the doctrine of this sermon is that the liberty one takes for himself he should accord his neighbor.[2]

The very next year, 1749, Tennent published his famous *Irenicum*. In his Nottingham sermon his one aim had been the reformation of the church and the triumph of the new evangelism. He was then unjustly severe upon the critics of the revival. Now the reunion of the Old

---

[1] How earnest was the effort of the presbytery of New Brunswick to come to amicable relations with the Old Side men is shown by their action in 1746 in relation to Maidenhead and Hopewell. A committee headed by Gilbert Tennent was appointed, with four ministers of the presbytery of New York as correspondents, to confer with Pastor Guild and the congregations of both sides for the purpose of effecting a union. The Presbyterian population of the two townships did not admit of the adequate maintenance of so many churches, and it would have been a distinct gain to the old congregations to receive the warm, new blood of the evangelical party. The state feeling did not permit reunion at this time, but it was effected a few years later. This friendly attitude of the New Sides in 1746 was in sharp contrast with the hostility toward them manifested by the synod of Philadelphia in its letter of that year to Rector Clap, of Yale College. MS Minutes of the New Brunswick Presbytery for May 21, 1746.

[2] Gilbert Tennent, *Brotherly Love Recommended*.

Sides and the New Sides was the single object in his range of vision, and he minimized the differences between the two parties, going to the opposite extreme. He would have his readers believe that the differences between the two sides were over mere circumstantials in discipline and over divergent estimates of the number of genuine conversions in the revival.[1]

One concession made by Tennent in the *Irenicum* shows how confused even the evangelicals sometimes were concerning a practice which was a necessary application of their fundamental principle of conversion. He disavows the authority of the church to judge the "inward experiences" of those who seek admission to membership in the church or participation in the Lord's Supper.[2] In this he failed to follow the example of his teacher, Frelinghuysen. Jonathan Edwards attained the advanced position at about the same time that Tennent published his *Irenicum*, and thereby Edwards lost his church at Northampton in the following year, but his courage ultimately saved Congregationalism from the blight of rationalism.[3] Had Tennent been logical, he would in addition have denied the authority to judge the gracious experiences of candidates for the ministry, but this would have been the surrender of one of the main contentions of the evangelicals.

In the year of the *Irenicum*, 1749, the synod of New York made proposals of union to the synod of Philadelphia. These were cordially received, but in the subsequent exchange of plans the old synod held out stiffly for impossible concessions, while the new synod insisted upon the annulment of the protestation of 1741, and it urged some recognition of the revival as a glorious work of God. Thereupon the synod of Philadelphia declared that the protestation was made upon justifiable grounds, and its members were not in the least convinced that the synod had taken a wrong action in relation to it. So far from recognizing the revival they suggested the propriety of the synod of New York pointing out what was the work of God and what were the artifices of Satan in the late religious appearances.[4]

The reply of the synod of New York, prepared by a committee of which Gilbert Tennent was chairman, was framed to smooth the ruffled spirits of the conservatives and continue the negotiations at a time when the difficulties in the way of reunion appeared to be insuperable. The

[1] Gilbert Tennent, *Irenicum*, pp. 84, 99.

[2] *Ibid.*, pp. 26, 27.

[3] Dwight, *Edwards*, p. 298; Allen, *Jonathan Edwards*, p. 263.

[4] *Records of the Presbyterian Church*, pp. 237, 193, 239, 195, 242, 199, 202, 245, 205.

old synod maintained that the protestation, being made by individual members, could not be disannulled by the synod itself. The new synod saw in this answer the suggestion of a possible solution of the knotty problem. It proposed that the protestation be disavowed as a synodical act and be regarded henceforth as only the act of its signers as individuals. In the interest of peace this concession was finally made. Then in the assurance that union was at hand the synod of New York appointed its meeting for the year 1758 at Philadelphia. A joint committee of both bodies prepared a plan of union which was adopted by the synods, thus happily ending the schism which had been made in 1741 by the irregular expulsion of the active promoters of the revival. Great was the triumph of Gilbert Tennent to be the first moderator of the newly organized synod of New York and Philadelphia, holding its first meeting in his church at Philadelphia.[1]

The plan of union was conceived in a spirit of fairness and friendliness. In the debate between the New Sides and the Old Sides the former had made a distinction between determinations of the synod in doctrine and government which might properly be regarded as indispensable and those in which forbearance might well be exercised toward tender consciences. They did not think that agreement in every truth and duty should be made a term of communion. This principle was adopted in the plan. A protestation was defined in the agreement between the synods as a solemn appeal from the bar of a judicatory to God against a public determination of that judicatory with which the protestor's conscience was offended. The implication was that the famous protestation of 1741, which was now disavowed as a synodical act, was altogether irregular. Provision was made against intrusion, but it was considered unbrotherly for a minister to refuse his pulpit to a regular member of the synod. The examination of candidates for the ministry as to their learning and experimental acquaintance with religion was committed to the presbyteries, and nothing was said of synodical examination and college diplomas. This was a complete surrender to the original contention of the presbytery of New Brunswick.[2]

In this agreement the members of the synod of New York reaffirmed their adherence to their former sentiments in favor of the late religious appearances, and the united synod made an unequivocal declaration in favor of the evangelical principles which the New Sides had held forth. When men bewail their sins, choose Christ for their Savior, and make it

[1] *Ibid.*, pp. 250, 251, 116, 267, 221, 275, 279, 224, 230, 284.

[2] *Ibid.*, pp. 253, 286, 287.

the business of their lives to please God and to do good to their fellow men, this is to be acknowledged as a glorious work of God, even though it be attended with unusual bodily commotions through the infirmity of some of its subjects. But when persons judge themselves converted because of visions, voices, and faintings and do not give the evidence of a changed life, such persons are believed to be under a dangerous delusion. The members of both synods engaged to promote such a work of grace as their united testimony had thus described, to pursue spiritual and awakening methods, and to cultivate harmony among themselves and piety among the people. Though the Old Side ministers retained their unfavorable opinion of the Great Awakening, they were now thoroughly committed to its aims.[1]

The most eloquent testimony to the triumph of the evangelical party is given by the increase in the number of ministers during the period of separation. In 1741, at the time of the schism, there were forty-three ministers in the synod of Philadelphia, including the absent members.[2] Of this number nine were excluded, but not more than seven may properly be regarded as constituting the New Brunswick party. In 1745, when the synod of New York was organized, the Old Side synod numbered twenty-five and the New Side synod twenty-two. Among these twenty-two New Side ministers the New Brunswick party had increased from seven to thirteen.[3] In 1758, when the reunion was effected, the Old Side synod numbered twenty-two and the New Side synod seventy-two, so that in the united synod the evangelical party was more than three times as numerous as the conservative.[4]

This gain is not to be explained by a comparison of the Presbyterian immigration from New England with that from Ulster, for upon this basis a greater proportionate growth of the conservative church might be expected. The Great Awakening itself supplies the only sufficient answer. Many of the ministers of the synod of Philadelphia were old men. The recruits from abroad were sometimes morally unfit, and sometimes they were discouraged by the hard conditions of colonial life. Much the same may be said of the candidates prepared in the schools of the conservatives in the colonies. The losses of the synod were therefore great. On the other hand the young enthusiasts of the synod of New York were in many instances soon worn out by their constant itinerations and the heedless expenditure of their powers. John Rowland,

---

[1] *Records of the Presbyterian Church*, pp. 287, 288.

[2] *Ibid.*, pp. 147, 153, 159.   [3] *Ibid.*, pp. 175, 232.

[4] *Ibid.*, pp. 228, 280, 285.

William Robinson, Samuel Blair, and Samuel Davies all died young. The New Side churches were active, growing, and full of young people. The heroism of these leaders and others like them attracted splendid young men to take their places. The synod therefore grew in spite of its losses.[1]

Though the conservatives and evangelicals came together upon an evangelical platform, the two parties still existed, with their sharply contrasted programs. The conservative minority, which had proudly waved the banner of synodical authority when it was in control of the synod, now resisted that authority, and a permanent rupture was prevented by practically allowing the conservatives to put their own interpretation upon the Directory and the Articles of Union. The center of disturbance now, as in 1741, was in the presbytery of Donegal, where alone the conservatives were in the majority.[2] The divisions in the congregations in that region were not healed in 1758 and in some instances continued to the close of the century. This long-drawn-out bitterness is attributed by the historian of the presbytery of Donegal to "honesty of convictions and characteristic Scotch-Irish obstinacy."[3]

Though we cannot accept Gilbert Tennent's exaggerated representation of the essential agreement of the two parties, for there were fundamental differences between them, his action and that of the majority demonstrate the fact that the Great Awakening was not so much a dividing as a unifying force in the realm of religion, and, whether dividing or unifying, it was a force. From the point of view of more developed American Protestantism the failure to insist on regenerate church membership may be criticized, but the evangelicals must be praised for not founding a separate church upon a too restricted test of what constitutes regeneration. The two parties still existed. The one was Methodistic in its emotional warmth and propagating zeal, in its advocacy of moral reform, and in its humanitarian spirit. The other party was described by non-Presbyterians as being quite the opposite in each of these particulars.[4] No doubt there were endless shadings between them; but it was the dominant evangelical party that gave the Presbyterian Church its

[1] Webster, *A History of the Presbyterian Church*, p. 251; Hodge, *Constitutional History of the Presbyterian Church*, Part II, p. 210.

[2] *Records of the Presbyterian Church*, pp. 317, 319, 321, 330, 344, 347–50, 355–60, 366, 371, 372, 383–85.

[3] West in *Centennial Memorial of the Presbytery of Carlisle*, I, 93.

[4] Smith, *Life and Letters of James Osgood Andrew*, p. 30.

influence in colonial society. Though both sides, true to their Presbyterian training, advocated military defense, it was the New Side leaders who were the more active in calling men to arms in times of crisis, thus overcoming Quaker opposition.[1] Though both sides inherited an aversion to the Church of England, it was the New Side propagandists that came into actual collision with it in the several provinces.[2] Furthermore, in New York they resented the diversion to a Church institution of funds raised for a provincial college. It was their friend Whitefield whose application for a college charter in Georgia was negatived by the British authorities because he refused to accept a charter modeled upon King's College.[3] The synod, now controlled by the evangelicals, united with the Congregationalists in concerted measures to oppose the imposition of bishops upon the American Colonies.[4] The Anglican church was looked upon as the handmaid of the Anglican government. It was easy to transfer their resentments from the church to the government. Gilbert Tennent extolled limited monarchy as the ideal government, for as a Presbyterian he hated democracy and as a son of Ireland he dreaded tyranny.[5] The Presbyterians loudly protested their loyalty to the king, but they feared the designs of the English government to deprive them of their constitutional liberty. When at last the Revolutionary War came, the Presbyterian ministers of the Middle Colonies outnumbered all others combined.[6] They were still prevailingly New Side. It was the Great Awakening that gave the church this splendid body of leaders. The ministers had trained the people of their churches till they were an intelligent, resolute, aggressive host for the defense of their ecclesiastical and political privileges. At their schools the youth of the land had imbibed evangelical principles in religion and an American program in politics. It was the Great Awakening that swept into their churches and welded together such seemingly discordant elements as were then included in the population of the Middle Colonies.

[1] Franklin, *Autobiography*, p. 136; Gilbert Tennent, *The Late Association for Defence Encouraged, The Late Association Further Encouraged,* a third publication of 182 pages on same subject, *Sermon for Day of Fasting and Prayer,* and *Sermon before Capt. Vanderspiegel's Company;* Brainerd, *The Life of John Brainerd,* pp. 311–14; West, *op. cit.,* I, 71–85; Watson in *Centennial Memorial of the Presbytery of Carlisle,* II, 167–69.

[2] Miller, *Rodgers,* p. 105.

[3] Whitefield, *A Letter to his Excellency Governor Wright.*

[4] Miller, *op. cit.,* p. 185.

[5] Gilbert Tennent, *A Sermon on Occasion of Victory, Funeral Sermon for Captain Grant,* and *Danger of Persecution.*

[6] Briggs, *American Presbyterianism,* p. 343.

2. *Triumphant evangelism in the Dutch Reformed Church.*—There is a remarkable parallelism between the history of the Church of Scotland in America and that of the Netherlandish church here, for both were presbyterian in polity and Calvinistic in creed. But every difference between the two parties in the Dutch church, the conservative and formalist on the one hand and the evangelical and progressive on the other, was carried to exaggeration. The development was slower in the Dutch church than in the Presbyterian, though Frelinghuysen had early introduced the new teaching.

Revivalists in the Dutch church, as in the Presbyterian, sought out promising candidates for the ministry, superintended their studies, and then united in practical measures to induct them into office without actual violation of the rules of the church. The founder of ministerial education among the Dutch was Domine Dorsius, a friend of Frelinghuysen and a neighbor of William Tennent, of the Log College.[1] Dorsius prepared a number of young men for the Dutch ministry, the first of whom, John Henry Goetschius,[2] was to become after Frelinghuysen the leading promoter of the Great Awakening among the Dutch. At the completion of his studies a call was presented to the young candidate by the churches of Queens county, Long Island.[3] They had waited nine years in vain for a minister from Holland. Now Dorsius and Frelinghuysen ordained Goetschius, and in April, 1741, he was installed by Domine Freeman.[4]

Was the ordination of Goetschius valid? Dorsius based his authority in part upon the indefinite charge committed to him in Holland. His main reliance was upon the teaching of Voetius "that in a country where there was no synod or classis one minister might make another."[5] It had been the custom of the trading companies to look to the classis of Amsterdam for ministers who were desired from time to time for the foreign plantations. Out of this custom had grown the ecclesiastical jurisdiction of this presbytery over all the foreign possessions of the Netherlands. Even after New York was lost to the Dutch politically this ecclesiastical relation continued.[6] One or two German Reformed ministers of Pennsylvania owned the jurisdiction of this classis over them.[7] The classis did not think it possible that an adequate education

---

[1] *Ecclesiastical Records of New York*, p. 2701.

[2] *Ibid.*, pp. 2684, 2833, 2837; *Records of the Presbyterian Church*, p. 131.

[3] *Eccl. Rec. of New York*, p. 2743.   [4] *Ibid.*, p. 2752.   [5] *Ibid.*, p. 2782.

[6] *Ibid.*, p. 2826; Gunn, *Memoirs of the Rev. John H. Livingston, D.D.*, p. 82.

[7] *Eccl. Rec. of New York*, pp. 2478, 2484.

could be obtained in the colonies, and therefore, with the greatest reluctance, from time to time it appointed ministers in the colonies as a committee of the classis to examine and ordain candidates. But each time the classis protested that the permission was not to be regarded as a precedent, and that the request ought not to be made again.[1] The classis had not shown a friendly disposition to Frelinghuysen and his evangelical associates. Therefore Dorsius and Frelinghuysen, both independent and aggressively evangelical, exercised a power which seemed to be granted by the acknowledged text-books and by the necessity of the churches, and which was not without support in the canons of Dordecht. This bold action and the fear of the loss of its jurisdiction no doubt led the classis to authorize the ordination of a number of the students of Dorsius, Goetschius, and other ministers. Most of these young men were ardent supporters of the revival.

At first Goetschius was the admired pastor of all the elements of his several congregations, but when his deep interest in spiritual religion became apparent to all, and the work of conversion began as it had under the preaching of Frelinghuysen in the Valley of the Raritan, opposition closed in upon the young man from every side. Boel, of New York, directed the course of the disaffected, as he had done in the troubles of Frelinghuysen.[2] Goetschius was a powerful and successful preacher. He won the hearty support of the neighboring Presbyterian pastors.[3] When Ritzema came from Holland to New York City, free from bias, he was enabled to write to the classis in commendation of Goetschius.[4] It was impossible for the classis to recognize the validity of an ordination which was clearly an assumption of independence. For the sake of peace Goetschius yielded to the authority of the classis, which after interminable delays gave judgment that he was to be regarded only as a candidate, and that after his call by any church outside of Queens county the newly organized coetus was authorized to ordain him as pastor.[5] He was promptly called to Hackensack, reordained, and again New Jersey became the center of evangelical influence and ministerial training.[6]

The coetus, an inchoate classis or presbytery, was organized by a number of the Dutch ministers in the year 1747, with the long-delayed approval of the classis of Amsterdam.[7] The main purpose of several of

[1] *Eccl. Rec. of New York*, pp. 2468, 2673.

[2] *Ibid.*, pp. 2777, 2781, 2798, 2885.

[3] *Ibid.*, p. 2882.

[4] *Ibid.*, p. 2913.

[5] *Ibid.*, pp. 2842, 2939.

[6] *Ibid.*, p. 3027.

[7] *Ibid.*, p. 2974.

the pastors was to expedite the ordination of ministers trained in this country. They hoped ultimately to transform the coetus into a classis and to establish a college in America. The Dutch in the two provinces were increasing in numbers and wealth. The revival spreading among them sent many young men to prepare for the ministry in the schools established here and there in the studies of evangelical pastors. But the classis became more and more reluctant to permit their ordination unless they crossed the ocean to complete their studies in Europe. The Dutch church order, the classis affirmed, required of candidates the certificate of professors and two years' university residence.[1] When finally the proposition of an American classis and college was presented to the classis of Amsterdam and the synod of North Holland, the answer was that an American classis was an impossibility, for what authority could it possess in a land where the decisions of church courts were not enforced by the civil government? The thought of a Dutch college in America was an "airy castle," for where was its treasury, they asked, and what professors would teach in it?[2] In vain did Theodore Frelinghuysen, son of the founder of the evangelical party, attempt to show that the Presbyterians, belonging to the Reformed family of churches, maintained their presbyteries and synods and had erected a college with the aid of their British sympathizers.[3]

While the evangelicals and moderate conservatives associated themselves together in the coetus, the extreme conservatives, like Boel, of New York, refused to join it, even when urged to do so by the classis itself. They preferred to be in direct subordination to the classis, alleging that the coetus would lead to independence. They asserted that the church was in danger of being deluged with half-educated ministers.[4]

[1] *Ibid.*, pp. 2935, 2956.

[2] Meeting of coetus (*ibid.*, pp. 3490, 3493); withdrawal of city churches (*ibid.*, pp. 3495, 3497, 3499); Ritzema's reasons (*ibid.*, pp. 3505, 3518, 3532); Dutch professorship (*ibid.*, pp. 3506, 3515-17, 3542, 3554, 3557, 3574, 3613); convention (*ibid.*, pp. 3541, 3546, 3551, 3561); reply to petition of convention (*ibid.*, pp. 3566, 3636, 3656).

[3] *Ibid.*, pp. 3610, 3648, 3672, 3674, 3738, 3739, 3750, 3751, 3761. Four sons of the elder Frelinghuysen studied in this country and then went to Holland for the required two years. Upon their return Theodore became the eloquent preacher at Albany, and John succeeded his father in three of the Raritan churches, but two sons died on the return voyage. John petitioned the classis to permit the ordination of Henricus, his youngest brother, without requiring him to encounter the dangers of a voyage, but the appeal was denied. Theodore, having gone to Holland as the representative of the coetus and convention, also was lost on the return voyage. Henricus was finally ordained by the coetus without the consent of the classis.

[4] *Ibid.*, pp. 2798, 2999.

The actual danger of the Dutch church was its extinction through the loss of its young people, since many congregations were unable to obtain ministers from Holland. This party was increased in 1755 by the opposers of the revival who then withdrew from the coetus in consequence of the efforts to establish an American classis and college. They took the name of the "Conferentie."[1] Upon the apparent collapse of the coetus several of the conservative ministers intruded upon the fields of other pastors, responding to the calls of the disaffected. The suppressed antipathy to the principles of the Great Awakening suddenly burst into flame, and one of the most deplorable chapters in the history of the Dutch church was opened.[2] Thus the schism which was effected in the Presbyterian Church in 1741 was delayed in the Dutch church until 1755. In the one the opponents of the Great Awakening irregularly excluded the active promoters of the revival; in the other the conservative minority withdrew and organized a rival body, though both the coetus and the Conferentie professed subordination to the classis of Amsterdam.

Nowhere was the struggle between the evangelicals and conservatives more vital to the future character of the Dutch church than in the collegiate churches of New York City. The conservatives emphasized ritual and formal profession; they clung to the dependence on Holland and the Dutch language. The evangelicals held the conception of religion which was now dominant in the Presbyterian Church, and they proposed the establishment of English preaching in the Dutch churches. The consistory gave a call to an English minister in Holland, Archibald Laidlie. His preaching in New York was so popular and attended by so many conversions that the opposers of revivalism raised a hue and cry against him. One of his co-pastors led the opposition. The consistory was sued at law, but the decision of the court was against the complainants. An overwhelming majority of the members sustained the consistory. So great was the rage of many of the disaffected that they went over to the Church of England.[3]

The lapse into formality and the loss of the young were arrested to such a degree that another English preacher was demanded. Dr. John H. Livingston, a native of the province then pursuing postgraduate studies at the University of Utrecht, was called. He had come under the spell of the Great Awakening in his youth. Fervor, wisdom, and

---

[1] *Eccl. Rec. of New York*, pp. 3582, 3589, 3597.

[2] *Ibid.*, pp. 3540, 3548, 3608, 3624, 3644.

[3] Gunn, *op. cit.*, pp. 99–109, 131–55.

courtesy made him the pacificator of the troubled churches of his faith. The schism in the Dutch church lasted from 1755 to 1772. Livingston brought a plan of union which the classis of Amsterdam had approved. Every claim for which the coetus had so long struggled was at last conceded. Under this plan a synod and five classes were organized to meet the requirements of the now expanded Dutch church.[1] Livingston was afterward the president of the college for which Theodore Frelinghuysen had died, of which Hardenbergh, the student of John Frelinghuysen, was the founder.[2] Livingston was the exponent of the doctrines of the Frelinghuysens, the Tennents, and Whitefield, and he lived to see these doctrines cherished throughout the communion.

Thus the Great Awakening saved the Dutch church from becoming a ritualistic passageway to the Church of England. The revival as a continuing force brought the Dutch church into its more natural position of fraternal correspondence with the Presbyterian Church. Thus it became charged with the same religious spirit, adopted the same political tenets, and was able to take a pronounced stand in favor of the American cause in the Revolutionary War. The wealth, influence, and strategic position of the Dutch gave significance to this stand of their church.

3. *Pietism versus conservatism in the German Reformed Church.*— The history of the German Reformed Church in the Middle Colonies is that of the familiar contest between two parties, one pietistic and one conservative, and the contest leading to schism.

In the year 1744 Domine Dorsius, of Neshaminy, in behalf of the synods of Holland, entered into negotiations with the Presbyterian synod of Philadelphia with a view to a union of Presbyterians, German Reformed, and Dutch Reformed. The synod was now controlled by the Old Sides, who were naturally adverse to organic union, but they did express their willingness to join in measures of mutual assistance.[3] As late as 1750 the synod of North Holland was still favorable to the union of the three Reformed bodies in America, but in 1751 it came to a different determination. A report from the colonies had come to the synod that "the Scotch presbytery," meaning the synod of Philadelphia, was

[1] *Ibid.*, pp. 197–205, 221–40.

[2] All five sons of T. J. Frelinghuysen died within ten years of the death of their father. Only one, John, left a son. From him is descended the honored New Jersey family. John established a theological school at Somerville, New Jersey. One of his students, J. R. Hardenbergh, was his successor in the pastorate and was the first president of Queens College, incorporated in 1770, and later known as Rutgers. Messler, *Memorial Sermons*, pp. 181–91.

[3] *Records of the Presbyterian Church*, p. 174; Briggs, *op. cit.*, p. 284.

"not only entirely independent, but without forms of doctrine and liturgies." When it is remembered that the Old Sides were sticklers for orthodoxy and precedent, it is ridiculous enough to read of their synod "that neither now, nor ever, can one be sure of its opinions."[1] Dorsius was an evangelical, but now German conservatives had the ear of the Dutch authorities.[2]

These words of censure may have had an innocent origin in the purpose of an active missionary not to permit the Holland authorities to resign their responsibilities to a sister Reformed body in the colonies which was still in its infancy and torn by strife. Whether the author of the criticism or not, such a missionary was Michael Schlatter, who, as representative of the synods of Holland, organized a German coetus in 1747. He had but four associates in the service of a German Reformed population of thirty thousand. His energy in organizing congregations was remarkable. In Europe he collected a large contribution for the support of the work in Pennsylvania, and upon his return to America brought a number of young ministers, Otterbein, who was to become the leader of the evangelicals, among them. Church people in England became interested in his appeal and raised an immense sum for the establishment of charity schools among the Germans. Schlatter was made the superintendent of these schools. The published statements of the English advocates of the scheme greatly offended the Germans of Pennsylvania when they were reported in the province. The project was believed to have a political bearing and to pave the way, in the purpose of its managers, for the establishment of the Church of England. The Germans spurned the foreign charity, following the lead of the Dunker Saur rather than the hesitating encouragement given the schools by Reformed and Lutheran pastors.[3]

Thus the spirit of conservatism among the Germans isolated this people from both the Scotch-Irish Presbyterians and the English churchmen and aroused that hostility to the English language and to education which was long a barrier to the progress of culture in Pennsylvania. Nevertheless the revival of religion was a powerful ferment among the people, for Pietism was itself a German product. The Germans in spite of themselves were also acted upon by English-speaking promoters of the revival. In the coetus of the Reformed Church Otterbein was

---

[1] *Eccl. Rec. of New York*, pp. 2874, 3165.

[2] Dorsius broke down through drink and left the colonies about 1748. Corwin, *Manual*, p. 244; *Eccl. Rec. of New York*, p. 3138.

[3] *Ibid.*, pp. 2960, 2984; Dubbs, *The Reformed Church, German*, p. 287.

the leader of the Pietists against the more numerous conservatives. In the religious destitution of the German people the partisans of Otterbein advocated sending out evangelists to win the people to Christ. They were willing to waive the usual educational requirements if candidates showed piety and ability. The conservatives placed all dependence on the church school and the stated religious services. Upon the suggestion of Superintendent Asbury, of the Methodist conference, and under the leadership of Otterbein the class system was introduced into a large number of German Reformed churches. These classes were like the Methodist societies in the Church of England and the *collegia pietatis* in the churches of the fatherland. The conservatives opposed this movement strenuously and finally excluded one of the class leaders. A new denomination, known as the United Brethren, was then organized. Otterbein remained in the Reformed Church, but like Wesley he gave ordination to the preachers of the new church. The coetus became extremely conservative, while the United Brethren did a work among the Germans like that of the Methodists among the English.[1] As in other instances where the Great Awakening led to schism, the evangelistic church in time became the more numerous.

4. *Triumphant Pietism in the Lutheran Church.*—The foregoing brief account of the German Reformed suggests a similar treatment of the Lutherans, for in Germany these denominations were sister state churches, and in America their early history was strangely interwoven.

Muhlenberg is known as the father of the Lutheran Church in America because he was the organizer of the denomination, not the first Lutheran minister. He came to Pennsylvania in 1742 as a missionary from the Orphan House at Halle. He found the group of congregations which he was to serve and the Lutheran population of the province in general to be "needy emigrants and a people scarcely recovered from long servitude."[2] They had not the means to build churches and schools and to support ministers. This was their own thought, at least, and accordingly they left the support of their missionaries to the fathers at Halle. Muhlenberg was a Pietist in the true sense and earnestly sought for the conversion of his hearers. He often found that the Lutherans who had come under Moravian influence gave greater evidence of piety than those who had indignantly resisted the Moravians; but he abhorred the custom of some members of the brotherhood who intruded upon Lutheran churches under the guise of Lutheran ordination. On the

[1] *Ibid.*, p. 312.

[2] Jacobs, *The Lutherans*, pp. 218, 254.

other hand he was himself despised by the conservatives of his own communion as a Pietist and a heretic from the scorpion nest at Halle. Like Spener and Francke, he was loyal to the standards of his church, but he sought to lead the people to a deeper spirituality and more Christian conduct. He did not exclude the unconverted from the Lord's table or from the eldership in the churches, but he strove earnestly for their conversion. The destitute Lutherans of Pennsylvania began to lift up their heads.

As churches were built for the congregations which originally called Muhlenberg and schools were opened where grown youths learned their letters, the young missionary began to extend his itinerations to the pastorless congregations of his communion. Soon there arrived from Halle additional pastors and catechists. In 1748 the synod, or ministerium, of Pennsylvania was organized by four missionaries from Halle, one other German, and one Swedish minister, and a large number of lay delegates from different parts of the province.[1] In 1760 the synod was reorganized upon a broader basis than that of the Halle missionaries and their closest friends. The master spirit was still Muhlenberg, whose itinerations extended from New York to Georgia.[2]

While the founder of the Lutheran Church in America sharply criticized the blurring of denominational lines as illustrated in the mission of Zinzendorf in Pennsylvania, he had drunk too deeply of Pietism at Halle not to show much of the same catholic spirit. He and the ministers trained at Halle felt kindly toward Whitefield, for had not the evangelist upon his first return to England taken collections for the Lutheran Salzburgers? As late as 1770 the great orator preached in Muhlenberg's church to a crowded auditory and then took occasion to honor Francke, who had so greatly influenced his own career. The relations of the Lutherans and the Episcopalians were peculiarly intimate. It was reported to the bishop of London that there were sixty-five thousand Church people in Pennsylvania, including forty thousand Lutherans "who reckon[ed] their service the same as that of the Church." Some of the Lutheran ministers, like General Muhlenberg, son of the founder, accepted episcopal ordination, intending thereby not to leave the Lutheran ministry but to obtain greater legal privileges in some of the colonies.[3]

This emphasis upon a common Christianity, so generally characteristic of the evangelicals of that period, was illustrated by the intercourse

[1] Jacobs, *The Lutherans*, p. 243.
[2] *Ibid.*, p. 258.   [3] *Ibid.*, p, 283.

of the Halle missionaries with other denominations. With Michael Schlatter, superintendent of the German Reformed churches, Muhlenberg entered into hearty co-operation for the religious development of the German settlers. Sometimes they held union services, as Frelinghuysen and Tennent had done at New Brunswick. Muhlenberg was particularly friendly with the Tennents and other New Side Presbyterians.[1]

Thus the men who gave character to the American Lutherans of the eighteenth century demonstrated the possibility of uniting the cultivation of a rich liturgy with the prosecution of a warm-hearted evangelism. While enduring hardship in the service of their own denomination they were first of all Christians.

5. *Methodism versus formalism in the Church of England.*—The Great Awakening, as promoted by Whitefield and later by the Wesleyan missionaries from England, did not have the quickening effect upon the Church of England in the colonies that Pietism, as promoted by Muhlenberg and other missionaries from Halle, had upon the sister ritualistic church. Whitefield, like Spener and Francke in Germany, had not the slightest desire to lead a separation from the church.[2] He lived and died a priest of the Church of England.[3] Whitefield accepted the Thirty-nine Articles in their literal and original meaning, in this differing from the greater part of the clergy of his day. He was warmly attached to the ritual, without ridiculously imposing it upon non-ritualistic congregations whenever invited to preach in their meeting-houses. In the cities of New York and Philadelphia and in the southern provinces he contributed to the growth of the Presbyterian and Baptist denominations, for great numbers of Church people were won to the acceptance of evangelical doctrine and a stricter moral code because the evangelist was one of their own clergy. Then, finding that these doctrines were opposed by their own rectors, it was easy for numbers to follow the advice of their spiritual awakener to seek stimulating ministrations wherever they could be found.

The churchman thus undermined the power of the Church by putting religion before mere organization, or, better, not Whitefield but the clergy did this by failing to improve the supreme opportunity of their time to fulfil their proper function and, incidentally, to attach the people

---

[1] *Ibid.*, pp. 288, 289.

[2] Gledstone, *George Whitefield*, p. 219.

[3] *South Carolina Gazette*, February 13, 1742; January 6, May 5, 1746; Whitefield, *Letter to his Excellency Governor Wright;* Ravenel, *Eliza Pinckney*, pp. 21–24.

to their church.　Whitefield does not give a favorable view of the rectors of his time, yet the correspondents of the Society for the Propagation of the Gospel report that as the century advanced there was an improvement in the character of appointments.[1]　Dissenting ministers, educated in the colonies, who conformed, appear to have made the more efficient missionaries among the English-speaking people.　French and German Reformed and Lutheran ministers, now finding themselves subje[ct] the English government and oppressed by poverty, felt the attra[ction] of the English national church.[2]　In Virginia the contemporaneous c[or]ruption of the English church and state was reflected in the life of th[e] clergy.　Davies exhorted the clergymen of the establishment to preach the doctrines of the Thirty-nine Articles and, stimulated by the success of the Presbyterians, to lend a hand in the reclamation of the province.[3] Later in the century a Virginia rector wrote to John Wesley that of ninety-four ministers of the Church of England in the province ninety-three appeared to be without "the power and spirit of vital religion."[4] These Anglican clergymen in America looked to the English government for the advancement of their interests.　Their hostility to the Great Awakening and their outspoken Tory sympathies led to the collapse of their influence in the period of the Revolutionary War.[5]

At every period, however, there were clergymen here and there who braved the scorn of their associates and defended the principles and practices of the Great Awakening.　When Edwards' exaltation of the affections to the seat of honor in the religious life of thinking men had become the common possession of Protestant America, there were not wanting Episcopal clergymen who warmly accepted this philosophy. They preached the fundamental doctrines of Whitefield and Wesley. The low-church party shared with other parties in making the communion which first erected a Protestant altar in the colonies a power again in the spiritual training of the people.[6]

Whitefield had never attempted in the colonies to establish a society within the church, much less a separate church, to perpetuate his influence.　It was the genius of Wesley, however, to multiply himself by the

---

[1] *Eccl. Rec. of New York*, pp. 1551, 1609, 1883, 1892, 1899, 1906, 1909, 1917, 1951, 1991, 2014, 2096.

[2] *Ibid.*, pp. 1559, 1816, 1861.

[3] Davies, sermon on *Duties*, pp. 3, 4, 8–11.

[4] Year of 1773.　Tyerman, *Wesley*, III, 151.

[5] McConnell, *History of the American Episcopal Church*, pp. 180–89, 205–11.　It is convenient to cite this popular author, but the text is based on wider reading.

[6] *Ibid.*, p. 145.

organization everywhere of Methodist societies. As early as 1765 Methodist families emigrated to New York, and after a time Philip Embury began to preach. He was assisted by Captain Webb, who founded a society at Philadelphia. In response to an appeal to Wesley for help the conference in 1769 sent Boardman and Pilmoor to America. They preached to throngs. In two years the membership reached three hundred and sixteen.[1] In 1770 Wesley wrote to Whitefield, then making his last journey through the colonies, to beg him to encourage the Methodist preachers.[2] Afterward Jonathan Bryan, Whitefield's friend, wrote to Wesley that the evangelist's preaching was of unspeakable use to many, but as Whitefield's ministry was mostly in the populous districts the inhabitants of many parts were still in deplorable ignorance. Bryan pleaded for teachers for these people. His words referred especially to the Southern Provinces, and it was in them that the Methodist lay preachers under the leadership of the heroic Asbury had the most astonishing success.[3]

The Methodist society thus established in the colonies was within the Church of England, though condemned by the remnant of its clergy. It was a living, expanding society in a dying, unyielding church. The inevitable result followed, as in the Presbyterian, Dutch Reformed, and German Reformed denominations. In the period following the Revolutionary War thousands of members had been deprived of baptism and the Lord's Supper for years. Wesley saw but one way to prevent schism in his American conference. The bishop of London had blindly refused to ordain a Methodist preacher destined for the American states.[4] Then John Wesley exercised the right of an elder, as he had long conceived it, to join with other elders of the Christian church in ordaining men as ministers of the gospel for the Methodist societies in America. These ministers, upon their arrival in America, were to ordain Asbury and other lay preachers, making them elders like themselves. The superintendents, Coke and Asbury, were given the title of bishop by the headstrong Americans, but it was an episcopacy based upon presbyterian ordination.[5] The success of Methodism was not altogether due to the

[1] Tyerman, *op. cit.*, III, 47. Pilmoor eventually became rector of St. Paul's. Watson, *Annals of Philadelphia*, I, 455.

[2] Tyerman, *op. cit.*, III, 60.   [3] *Ibid.*, III, 116.

[4] "It is doubtful if any single action of a bishop has ever been more fruitful for evil than his refusal."—McConnell, *op. cit.*, p. 170.

[5] John Wesley, assisted by other ordained ministers of the Church of England, ordained Whatcoat and Vasey as presbyters, and he ordained Dr. Coke, who was already a presbyter of the Church of England, as superintendent. Tyerman, *op. cit.*, III, 426–38.

felicitous union of appropriate organization with fervent evangelism. Revivalism had already won the favor of the American people through the preaching of Edwards, Whitefield, Tennent, Davenport, Davies, and the Baptist evangelists. Asbury, at the head of his traveling preachers, entered into the apostolic succession of these American bishops.

6. *The changing policy of the Moravian brotherhood.*—Episcopacy and Methodism suggest that the Moravians be considered next in order. In Germany the Moravian Church had participated in the pietistic movement; in England, through Wesley, it was one of the sources of the Methodist Revival; in America Zinzendorf's itinerating "fishers" were successful propagators of the Great Awakening. No sooner had the one hundred and twenty immigrants settled in their frontier town of Bethlehem than they began to send out a very considerable portion of their number as itinerant evangelists. By 1748 there were thirty-one centers of such labor. One of these circuits embraced eighteen stations, others less. These itinerants from Bethlehem reached the extremities of the country in Georgia and Maine. The stupendous sacrifices of the Moravians in men and money were made possible by their zeal and semi-communistic system.[1]

In spite of the heroism of the brotherhood time wrought changes in its policy. Conferences, still called Pennsylvania synods, were held as late as 1748, although union with other denominations was no longer possible, for Muhlenberg had come to organize the Lutherans, and Schlatter, the German Reformed. The ideal of unity was noble, but the form of unity attempted was chimerical. This method of thought and activity was after a time condemned by the Moravians themselves and was abandoned. The Unity of the Brethren no longer in their thought included this Lutheran church member and that Reformed, for the Moravian brotherhood was now conceived of as quite a separate church. Their economic system made actual incorporation with them difficult. Even after this was given up their sufferings in the French and Indian War and the weight of debt which came upon them after the death of Zinzendorf hindered their evangelistic work and growth in numbers. Then the fear of being charged with proselytism drove them to the opposite extreme from their early practices, and they refused to employ the legitimate means by which the Methodists became a national blessing.[2] Yet by their Nazareth Hall they shared with other evangelical bodies in the honor of being pioneers in education.[3] Their train of

[1] J. T. Hamilton, *The Moravian Church in the United States*, p. 456.
[2] *Ibid.*, p. 469.　　　　[3] *Ibid.*, p. 466.

Indian mission stations from Connecticut to Alabama tells a wonderful story of sacrifice and success, of opposition and outrage. As the Moravians failed to do the work among the Germans which the Methodists were doing among the English, and as the so-called Sectarians were quite unable to meet the religious needs of the Germans on account of their peculiar and extra-Christian rules and usages, this task fell to new denominations not handicapped by outworn regulations and customs. Therefore the mission of the Moravians in part fell to the United Brethren, representing a union of progressive elements in the German Reformed and Mennonite denominations, and the Evangelical Association, another German Methodist church.

7. *The Baptists as revivers of the revival.*—The Baptist denomination was like the Moravians and the German Sectarians in that it was without the prestige of the national churches of the Old World transplanted in the New World. Even in Rhode Island it was not an established church, for it condemned the union of church and state. Everywhere in the colonies Baptists were looked upon as irregulars, by the conservatives at least, and classed with the Quakers of Pennsylvania and the Separates of Connecticut. At the present time the numerical strength of this communion is two or three times that of any of the national churches or of any denomination which possessed in the colonies the exceptional privileges of an established church. This change in relative popular following is a result of the Great Awakening. No denomination therefore owes more to the world-wide quickening than the Baptist, yet the churches of this communion, more generally than the Presbyterian and Congregational, in the beginning held aloof from the movement. The wonderful expansion of the denomination, when the mantle of Whitefield, Tennent, and Davenport had fallen upon its evangelists, came later than the period usually assigned to the Great Awakening. Baptist success belonged chiefly to the period following the Presbyterian revival in Virginia and antedated the early Methodist successes already recounted.

The baptism of fire that transformed this denomination was nevertheless a part of the Great Awakening, however weak were the Baptists in the beginning, and however hesitating was their adoption of the new methods. In the year 1740 and long afterward the Dunkers outnumbered in Pennsylvania the English-speaking Baptists.[1] In the Middle Colonies, as in other sections of the country, the Baptists were divided between Calvinists and Arminians, the former known as

---

[1] Benedict, *A General History of the Baptist Denomination*, II, 430-36; Vedder, *A History of the Baptists in the Middle States*, p. 75.

Particular Baptists and the latter as General Baptists. While the Presbyterians stormed over rules, precedents, and psalm-singing, the Baptists were no less at variance with each other over their interpretations of Scripture. Their churches were in a ferment over such questions as the Sabbath, laying on of hands, foot-washing, terms of communion, and psalm-singing.[1] It is true that a little group of five churches as far back as the year 1707 had organized the association of Philadelphia, the earliest Baptist association in the colonies. In stating the number as five the congregations at Pennypack and Philadelphia were treated as one church, the only one in the province. The others were scattered from Welsh Tract in Delaware and Cohansey in south New Jersey to Middletown in northeastern New Jersey.[2] Though the number of churches had increased to about twelve in 1740, what was that compared with the strength already attained in the Middle Colonies by the Presbyterians?[3] In 1742 the Philadelphia Confession was adopted. This confession was the model formula for associations subsequently organized. It was based upon the Westminster Confession and put the Baptists of the Middle Colonies in essential agreement with the foremost promoters of the revival.[4] While the Great Awakening itself brought a new subject of contention into the churches, it did not lead to a disruption of the association, for that body, being a league of independent churches, did not assume the legislative and judicial powers of a unified church, the assumption of which had led to the schism in the synod of Philadelphia. The Great Awakening turned the minds of the people from petty subjects of debate to questions of moment. The members of the churches who caught the spirit of the world movement gained a breadth of view and an evangelizing zeal which they had not known before.

While the memory of past wrongs tended to isolate the Baptists, religious fervor was native to many of their leaders and people. The Welsh preachers among them possessed in goodly measure the Keltic gifts which made Christmas Evans pre-eminent among British evangelists.[5] When Whitefield heard Jenkin Jones preach he pronounced him to be the only Philadelphia pastor who spoke "feelingly and with authority."[6] One of the young men baptized by Jenkin Jones was

---

[1] Vedder, *A History of the Baptists in the Middle States*, pp. 62, 66; Benedict, *op. cit.*, I, 581.

[2] *Ibid.*, I, 595; Vedder, *op. cit.*, p. 90.

[3] Benedict, *op. cit.*, II, 508–17.

[4] Vedder, *op. cit.*, p. 91.

[5] Benedict, *op. cit.*, I, 587.

[6] Whitefield, *Journal*, No. 6, p. 35.

Oliver Hart, who was a hearer of Whitefield and caught much of the spirit of pastor and evangelist. Hart went to Charleston and was the leader of the Baptists in their remarkable expansion in South Carolina after the death of Chanler, Whitefield's friend. Hart and William Tennent, a Presbyterian minister and son of William Tennent, of Freehold, were foremost supporters of the Revolution and itinerated in the interior of South Carolina under the appointment of the Committee of Safety, stirring up the people to the support of the patriot cause.[1]

Baptist history is continually interwoven with Presbyterian in the period of the Great Awakening and until the Revolutionary War. Abel Morgan, though educated by an Old Side Presbyterian minister,[2] was the first Baptist who was inspired by Whitefield's example to go upon extensive evangelistic journeys.[3] Hopewell, memorable for the revival under the leadership of Rowland, had also a Baptist church, in which were great ingatherings in the years 1747, 1764, and 1766.[4] The period frequently represented as deistic and religiously dead, when the people were distracted by war and political debate, was really marked by phenomenal revivals in a number of Baptist and Presbyterian churches. But it is true that there was no general religious excitement like that of 1740. John Gano, of Hopewell, a young Presbyterian, when troubled upon the subject of baptism after his conversion, resorted to one of the Tennents for advice. Tennent told him to think for himself and not to let the devil destroy his usefulness by indecision. Gano became one of the most eminent Baptist ministers of his generation. Few evangelists extended their itinerations over so many colonies and with such conspicuous success. Directly after his ordination in 1754 he was sent to South Carolina upon the solicitation of Oliver Hart. Whitefield was one of his hearers when he preached his first sermon at Charleston. In South Carolina the piety and eloquence of Gano were remarkably fruitful. Afterward he was the first pastor of the church in New York, was a chaplain in the Revolutionary army, and ended his career in Kentucky, where, though far advanced in years and partially paralyzed, he participated in the great Kentucky Revival, preaching with astonishing power. John Gano, orator and itinerant, linked together the Great Awakening and the Kentucky Revival.[5] One of the ministers whom Gano accom-

---

[1] Benedict, *op. cit.*, II, 139, 323–30.

[2] *Ibid.*, I, 564; Foote, *A Sketch of the Life of Rev. Abel Morgan.* In the Minutes of the Trenton Baptist Association, 1883.

[3] Whitefield, *Journal*, No. 6, p. 36.   [4] Benedict, *op. cit.*, I, 573.

[5] *Ibid.*, II, 306–23.

panied to Virginia before his ordination was Miller, of Scotch Plains. Miller was converted under the preaching of Gilbert Tennent. He, like Tennent, was a man of ardent piety who made friendships for life.[1] The career of another of the New Jersey pastors, Carman, of Hightstown, illustrates the ferment of the time. In his youth he was baptized into a Baptist church. In manhood he joined the Quakers. Then he went to the New Side Presbyterians. Finally he returned to the Baptists and was ordained to the ministry.[2] In the region that was profoundly stirred by Frelinghuysen and the itinerants of the presbytery of New Brunswick there were large accessions to Baptist churches. From this region Baptist evangelists went forth to proclaim the gospel in the most distant provinces.

In the neighboring province of Pennsylvania the Baptist success in New Jersey had no counterpart. Though the labors of the Dunkers were rewarded by frequent revivals among their fellow Germans, the regular Baptists had no rapid growth.[3] The sons of Ireland with few exceptions knew but one way to become religious, and that was the Presbyterian way. In New York, however, the growth of the Baptists was rapid, for into that province there was pouring a population of the dissatisfied and enterprising from New England. There was discrimination still in parts of New England against the Baptists and Separates, or Strict Congregationalists. The Separates fraternized with the Baptists, and the greater part coalesced with them. The remaining Separates in course of time reunited with the regular Congregationalists. It was in such a population that Drake, of New Canaan, first a Separate and then a Baptist, itinerated till he had gathered a church of nearly six hundred members scattered on both sides of the Hudson River. This unwieldy body was divided into five distinct churches.[4] Vermont, the Hudson Valley, and central New York were overrun by these immigrants from the older colonies. Baptist sentiment was strong among them, and frequent revivals built up the little Baptist churches which were established in the new country.[5]

We have seen that the Baptist preachers of New Jersey were to a considerable extent the heirs of Whitefield and the Log College men, and that the pioneers of the same denomination in New York were continuing the mission and methods of Davenport and the founders of the Shepherd's Tent. Like all other promoters of the Great Awakening,

[1] Benedict, *op. cit.*, I, 576.

[2] *Ibid.*, I, 575.

[3] Vedder, *op. cit.*, p. 75.

[4] Benedict, *op. cit.*, I, 549.

[5] Vedder, *op. cit.*, pp. 33–37.

they were described as purveyors of ignorance. It is true that they did not require a college diploma or its equivalent of candidates for the ministry, not unwisely barring from the pulpit men whose spiritual gifts and knowledge of the world fitted them for great usefulness in the ministry. Nevertheless the Baptists of the Middle Colonies who came under the influence of the New Side Presbyterians caught their enthusiasm for education. Private academies upon the model of the Log College were set up by several of the pastors.[1] The most famous of these was Eaton's academy at Hopewell, New Jersey, founded in 1756, where many preachers and representatives of other professions received their education. The Hopewell Academy stands in the same relation to Brown University as the Log College to Princeton.[2] James Manning, after studying at Hopewell and later at Princeton, where he was graduated, founded the College of Rhode Island in 1765.[3] Rhode Island was selected for the location of the college because Baptists were in control of the government in that colony, where alone a charter could be obtained. The prime movers in the founding and later in the endowing of the college were members of the association of Philadelphia. Manning also brought the First Baptist Church of Providence into the Calvinistic fold. Others of the Arminian order followed the example of the mother church. Thus the energies born of the Great Awakening led to the establishment of the first Baptist college and the practical unification of the churches under the banner of Calvinism.[4]

The itinerant evangelists of the Philadelphia association, such as Hart, Thomas, Miller, Van Horn, and Gano, achieved their greatest successes in Virginia and the Carolinas. In this they were like their predecessors, the New Side Presbyterians. Before the coming of these traveling preachers of the Middle Colonies and of Shubal Stearns, a

---

[1] As early as 1722 Abel Morgan, then pastor at Philadelphia, proposed to the association the establishment of an academy, hoping to obtain the assistance of Thomas Hollis, a London Baptist and the most liberal benefactor of Harvard College. Morgan's study at Middletown was a school, and so was that of Jenkin Jones, his successor at Philadelphia. Under the leadership of Jones the association raised money for a Latin grammar school at Hopewell under Isaac Eaton. Morgan Edwards, the successor of Jones, was the prime mover in the founding of the College of Rhode Island, Brown University. Keen, *The First Baptist Church of Philadelphia*, pp. 27–48. Rev. E. Kinnersly, the assistant of Jones, became a professor in the college at Philadelphia, and a later pastor of the same century, Dr. W. Rogers, was also a professor in the university. Benedict, *op. cit.*, I, 588.

[2] *Ibid.*, I, 573; II, 449.

[3] *Ibid.*, II, 443–48; Vedder, *op. cit.*, pp. 207–12. [4] *Ibid.*, p. 93.

Separate Baptist of Connecticut, there were General and Particular Baptists in Virginia, but their influence was a negligible quantity until ministers commissioned by the Philadelphia association adjusted their difficulties and filled them with evangelistic zeal. The church at Opeckon, after the visit of Stearns, went to such lengths of New Light emotionalism that some of the members lodged a complaint with the association of Philadelphia. Miller was sent to adjust the new difficulty, but he was so delighted with the experiences of these warm-hearted Christians that he expressed the wish that his own church-members were like them.[1] Thomas, prepared at Hopewell Academy, came to lead the regular Baptists of Virginia. Though he was assaulted by mobs, ruffians even attempting to take his life, the people came from great distances to hear him. The regulars, however, did not suffer the same degree of persecution as did the Separates, for some of their meeting-houses were licensed, and they were thought to be less enthusiastic than the Separates.[2]

The religious, social, and political revolution in Virginia and adjoining provinces was begun by the New Side Presbyterians of the Middle Colonies; the Philadelphia association of Baptists made a larger contribution, while in the end the Separate Baptists, originating in Connecticut, who finally united with the regular Baptists, furnished the greater number of voices, votes, and muskets. Shubal Stearns was a minister of the Separates who became a Baptist. He was without college training, like most of the Separates, because the Shepherd's Tent had been abolished by law, yet he was acquainted with men and books. Believing in the immediate teaching of the Spirit, he was strongly impressed that there was an important work for him in the distant west. He therefore led a bit of a colony to Opeckon, in the Valley of Virginia, and afterward to North Carolina. In 1755 a Separate Baptist church with sixteen members was constituted at Sandy Creek. This was the beginning of the Separate Baptist denomination in the South.[3]

To the surrounding population the principles and practices of the newcomers were grotesquely novel. To these North Carolinians the performance of certain outward duties was the sum of religion, for they were unacquainted with the ideas of conviction and conversion. Stearns's voice was so pathetic and his glance so penetrating that stories were told in that country of his power to enchant. Young men, drawn by curiosity

[1] Semple, *A History of the . . . . Baptists in Virginia*, pp. 375–77; Benedict, *op. cit.*, II, 23–28.

[2] *Ibid.*, II, 28–36; Semple, *op. cit.*, 378–85.   [3] *Ibid.*, pp. 13–16.

to his out-of-door meetings, fell to the ground and afterward became ministers. The sixteen members of the little church were increased to six hundred and six. The churches which grew out of this revival at Sandy Creek formed an association in 1758, the third organization of the kind, for the missionary labors of Oliver Hart in South Carolina had led to the formation of a second in 1751.[1]

Daniel Marshall was a lay preacher in the little church at Sandy Creek. He had been a deacon in New England, but he was set on fire by the preaching of Whitefield and became an exhorter. Believing that the millennium was about to dawn and that the Indians were the lost tribes of Israel, he penetrated the wilderness for their conversion without scrip or purse. He was rewarded with some degree of success, but war necessitated his removal. Then he joined Stearns in Virginia, became a Baptist, was licensed to preach, and later was ordained to the ministry. Marshall organized the first Separate Baptist church in Virginia. Among his converts were men of influence.[2] Then he moved to South Carolina where his one church became an association of Separate Baptist churches. At last he went to Georgia and established the Baptist cause there. Like many other Baptist preachers, Marshall suffered for his adherence to the Revolution.[3]

The spread of the new evangel was like fire in the Old Dominion. The men in power took alarm lest the old order of things should go down in a wave of democracy. Several preachers were arrested in Spottsylvania county as disturbers of the peace, for it was charged that they could not meet a man on the road without ramming a text of Scripture down his throat. While in prison at Fredericksburg, Waller and his associates preached through the grates to the people outside. The discharge, which came after long waiting, issued in a popular triumph. Now the preachers of water and fire carried their crusade into the older counties, for appeals came to them from all quarters. Mobs broke in upon their meetings. They suffered much as the Methodists were suffering in England. Yet their persecution won them friends in all classes. Larger and larger numbers of the sober common people were convinced by the burning words of the Baptist preachers and by their lives and trials, which attested to the truth of their teaching.[4]

The unlettered preachers who were thrown into the foul jails of the eighteenth century because they preached the gospel to the poor with

[1] Benedict, *op. cit.*, II, 366–68; Vedder, *op. cit.*, pp. 95–97.

[2] Semple, *op. cit.*, pp. 19–24; Benedict, *op. cit.*, II, 330–39.

[3] *Ibid.*, II, 350–55; Semple, *op. cit.*, pp. 16–19.   [4] *Ibid.*, pp. 24–42.

such alarming success turned upon their tormentors and charged the ministers of the establishment with ignorance of true religion and with the viclation of the rules of morality.   Whatever the measure of truth in these accusations, the accusers believed them and so did their hearers. More and more the established church was felt to be an appanage of monarchy, but the common people were becoming passionately republican.   The dissenters became so strong that the Revolutionary leaders, even when churchmen and members of the old aristocracy, were compelled to make concession after concession to them.[1]   The overthrow of the established church was the victory of the Baptists and Presbyterians. The regular Baptists supported the more numerous and aggressive Separate Baptists in their warfare on privilege.   After maintaining friendly relations for years they entered into union in the year 1787.[2]

Thus we have seen that in the Baptist denomination the supporters of the revival were few in 1740 and its critics many, but the revival gave its supporters such dynamic power that the denomination fairly leaped into a position of influence.   Impelled by the Great Awakening, the churches united under the creed of Whitefield and the leading promoters of experimental religion in the colonies.   It was the Great Awakening too that bestirred the Baptists to set up schools of higher learning.   Those who opposed these changes were either convinced of their error or left far behind to stagnate and disappear.   Those who felt the deepest, who threw discretion to the winds by giving full vent to their emotions, but who were at the same time thoroughly genuine, making every sacrifice for their religion, and who united fervor to the strictest morality then known—the Separate Baptists—made the greatest contribution to triumphant evangelism.   The history of this communion, as of all others considered in this chapter, illustrates the power of religion in society when belief, made red-hot by feeling, becomes faith.

[1] Semple, *op. cit..* pp. 43–54;   Benedict, *op. cit.*, II, 64–86.

[2] Semple, *op. cit.*, p. 99.

CHAPTER X

CONCLUSION

The purpose of this concluding chapter is to give a summary view of the boundaries, characteristics, and results of the evangelical revival, with special reference to its course in the Middle Colonies.

The Great Awakening has sometimes been represented as a tempest of ungoverned passions that swept over the colonies, leaving wreckage everywhere in the alienations and divisions in families, neighborhoods, and churches, the undermining of cherished institutions, and a relapse into indifference, debauchery, and irreligion.[1] An impartial study of the period, however, free from partisan and denominational bias, leads to a very different conclusion. It is that thousands and thousands[2] were given by the Great Awakening a new view of life's values, and from this view were derived new energies and new sympathies which gave direction not only to the subsequent career of these thousands but to the development of the whole American people. It was more than wave on wave of excitement; it was a transforming process in the nation's life.

The background of the international revival, of which the Great Awakening was a part, was the decadent civilization of the eighteenth century. The trend of the age was away from religion, away from the

---

[1] This is the burden of Charles Chauncy's *Seasonable Thoughts*. Chauncy was in sentiment a Universalist and was a particular friend of Mayhew, who was of pronounced Unitarian views. See Bradford's *Life of Dr. Mayhew*. F. M. Davenport, in his *Primitive Traits in Religious Revivals*, is led astray by the exaggerations of Chauncy. A reading of the two volumes of the *Christian History*, consisting of sober accounts by pastors of New England churches which came under the powerful influence of the revival, would correct an unfavorable view, but Professor Davenport seems not to have consulted these testimonies of the most eminent and pious ministers of New England.

[2] President Davies, of Princeton, referring to the power of the gospel in his student days, says: "I have seen thousands at once melted down under it, all eager to hear as for life, and scarcely a dry eye to be seen among them. Thousands still remain shining monuments of the power of divine grace in that glorious day" (Wesbter, *A History of the Presbyterian Church*, p. 550). Chapell, in *The Great Awakening of 1740*, gives an estimate of fifty thousand conversions in the Great Awakening, but the present writer makes no estimate, finding no definite basis for such attempt.

ideality, strenuousness, and rigor of a former time. A new period of moral laxity, religious indifference, and philosophic revolt had opened in Europe. These influences were quickly felt in the colonies, for every window was open toward the home lands, but there was little communication of ideas between the colonies. Though the colonies differed greatly from each other in their religious conditions, there were causes of religious decline in all peculiar to colonial life.

What was to be done to stem the tide of irreligion? The word "conservatism" sums up the answer of the majority of the sincerely religious. The conservatives of each denomination revered their own particular creed as the creation of a superior race of men, and therefore as a finality. Several of these denominations were national churches in the Old World. Therefore every reforming movement or spirit of change had to make headway against racial prejudices and veneration of ancestral faith. The customs of the past were invested with sanctity. Leaders sought to quarantine their people from the contagion of change. But the enthusiasm of the fathers could not be reproduced. The religion of the sons was without vitality and power.

Then it was that primitive Christianity sprang up in different parts of the world almost spontaneously, though generally there was an influence traceable to German Pietism. In the new teaching emphasis was not placed upon an inherited and formal profession, or upon the magic efficacy of ceremony, but upon an inner experience with its new passion for the service of God through the service of man. The seat of religion passed back from the head to the heart, and religion became again a force.

The Great Awakening in the Middle Colonies had several distinct sources. One of them was German Pietism. The revival at Germantown in 1722 may be selected somewhat arbitrarily as the date of the beginning of the Great Awakening among the Germans. Most assuredly the ministry of Frelinghuysen was an important source. His first ingathering in 1726 may be selected as the beginning of the Great Awakening among the Dutch. The establishment of the Log College in 1726, followed by the revivals of its early graduates in 1729 and 1732, was the third source, ranking second to none in the history of the Great Awakening in the Middle Colonies. This was the beginning of the revival among the Presbyterians. The Edwards revival of 1734 in its influence on New England men in the Middle Colonies was another source, evidenced by the revival at Newark in 1739. This influence in the Middle Colonies was cumulative, following and strengthening the earlier evangelical influences. The establishment of the Holy Club at Oxford and the coming of the Methodist evangelist to the Middle Colonies in 1739 were the fifth source of the Great Awakening in this section. It was then that the various streams united into a mighty river, a flood of flame, which swept over the country.

The name "Great Awakening" was especially appropriate to the Whitefield revival, which became powerful in the Middle Colonies and the coast region of the far southern provinces, and then in 1740 burst into astonishing flame in New England. A characteristic feature of the evangelical revival in this and in all lands was religious excitement, more intense than at any previous time since the Puritan Revival, and more widely extended than in any other religious movement since the Reformation. Waves of feeling, comparable to that seen in war or financial panic or political crisis, swept from community to community. The same phenomenon had appeared in the earlier Edwards revival, which began at Northampton and spread through western Massachusetts and Connecticut. Accordingly the name "Great Awakening" was applied in New England to these two waves of religious excitement. The subsequent Presbyterian and Baptist revivals in the South, the one beginning at Hanover in 1742 and the other at Sandy Creek in 1755, were in close dependence upon these earlier revivals and were quite as remarkable. Therefore they must be included in the four great revivals of the Great Awakening.

But the name must not be limited to the four most widespread excitements. Other revivals mentioned in the list of distinct sources of the Great Awakening in the Middle Colonies were certainly parts of it. There were many revivals in the Middle Colonies and in other sections, later than the Whitefield revival, which must be included, for they were all parts of the new religious quickening. Some were as late as the surprising outburst at Easthampton, Long Island, in 1764, under the pastorate of Samuel Buell.[1] Recognition must also be given to the early successes of the Methodists before the Revolutionary War. Some of the revivals of the various denominations were quite as phenomenal, though circumscribed in extent, and some were quite as important in their ultimate results as were the four great revivals. The Great Awakening is therefore best defined, not as successive waves of religious excitement, but as an intercolonial evangelical movement, part of the Methodist Revival in the empire and part of the world-wide Evangelical Revival.

---

[1] Buell, *A Faithful Narrative of the Remarkable Revival of Religion in the Congregation of Easthampton on Long Island.*

Whether the Great Awakening is conceived of as a remarkable effusion of the Holy Spirit, borrowing the description of its promoters, or as quickened religious activity, it was followed by a period of comparative stagnation. This first came to New England, then to the Middle Colonies, and finally to the South at the beginning of the Revolutionary War. When Whitefield gave a motto to the soldiers who sailed away with his friend Pepperrill to take Louisburg,[1] the significance of his act was that the New Englanders were now for a full half-century to turn their minds away from the exclusive attention to the affairs of religion which had occupied them during the progress of the revival. The earlier expeditions against the French did not command the same interest in the Middle Colonies that they did in New England, but the French and Indian War, the fierce debate with England, and the Revolutionary War combined with previous causes of religious decline to retard the progress of evangelism in the Middle Colonies, and finally in the whole country. There was, however, no section without occasional religious revivals. As a movement the evangelical revival never for a moment ceased to exist and to exert a powerful influence.

Having seen that the fundamental principle of the movement was the necessity of conversion and that the most striking characteristic was religious excitement, and having defined the boundaries in time, there remains to set in array other distinguishing marks of the Great Awakening. From the doctrine of the new birth there logically followed the belief in the divine guidance of the converted person, an assistance akin to inspiration. Evangelicals did not believe that their unaided intelligence could properly interpret the Bible, and in this they approached the Quaker position.[2] This reliance on divine guidance sometimes led to a whimsical following of impulses, impressions,[3] and the lot.[4] This

---

[1] Billingsley, *Life of the Rev. George Whitefield*, p. 245.

[2] Timothy Allen, for declaring "that the Bible could not, of itself, or by any man's efforts, do the unregenerate sinner any more good than the reading of an old almanac," was deposed from the Congregational ministry in 1741. Webster, *op. cit.*, p. 584; Fox, *Journal*, p. 72.

[3] Guidance through impulses and impressions constantly appear in the writings of Quakers, Pietists, Moravians, and Methodists. There were also Calvinists, like Davenport and Barber, who held this notion before coming under the influence of Whitefield. Jonathan Edwards opposed this dangerous tendency; his attitude toward this question became dominant among American Calvinists. Yet there were surprising instances of its recurrence, as when the learned Morgan Edwards, of Philadelphia, relying on a strong presentiment, prophesied in a sermon that he would die in the year 1770, but he lived till 1795. Keen, *The First Baptist Church of Philadelphia*, p. 49.

[4] Whitefield reproved Wesley for relying on the lot when he published a sermon against Calvinism. The Moravians employed the lot, and from them the early Methodists borrowed the custom. Tyerman, *Wesley*, I, 323.

extreme tendency in Whitefield and Davenport was soon corrected, but it has survived in certain circles to the present time.

To a measurably different attitude toward spiritual illumination from that entertained by conservatives was added a strikingly different attitude toward creeds. The evangelicals accepted the creeds of their respective denominations, but the tendency was to emphasize the fundamental agreement of the leading Protestant bodies and to treat the Bible alone as authoritative. They had closer sympathy with evangelicals of other denominations, respectively, than with opposers of the revival in their own. Therefore Whitefield was content to see his converts leave his own communion and join the Presbyterians and Baptists.[1] He was so true an exemplar of the spirit of this world movement that he founded no new sect.[2] It was only necessity, laid upon Wesley by conservatives, that drove him to a different course against his will.[3] Evangelism was a unifying principle in that it minimized accidental differences, while conservatism magnified them. Yet revivalism eventually led to various restatements of religious philosophy to give more adequate expression to the principles it had brought into prominence.[4]

It is sometimes represented that the unprecedented success of the Great Awakening, in the face of bitter opposition and in spite of serious defects in itself, was due to the Calvinistic doctrines preached throughout the colonies.[5] No doubt individual experiences of thousands were molded by the Calvinistic teaching in which they were drilled and by the form of that teaching employed by Whitefield, Tennent, and other leading evangelists. But the successful propagators of the revival in the colonies were not all Calvinists. The Moravians, Lutherans, and Methodists shared in it. When regarded as a world movement the success of the revival is clearly shown not to have been dependent upon any particular form of religious philosophy.

A more insistent question than creed was polity. Church government, as well as civil government, has its constitutional questions, and these were hotly debated in the period of the Great Awakening. The

---

[1] Whitefield, *Journal*, No. 6, pp. 23, 39.

[2] *New England Weekly Journal*, January 8, 1740; Whitefield, *Journal*, No. 6, p. 40.

[3] Tyerman, *op. cit.*, III, 436.

[4] The works of Jonathan Edwards and Joseph Bellamy are illustrations. Bellamy, *True Religion Delineated, or Experimental Religion*.

[5] This is the view of Hodge. See his *Constitutional History of the Presbyterian Church*, Part II, pp. 46–50.

conservatives were in the majority in the various denominations. The evangelicals were compelled to insist on the right of the individual to a wider liberty than the conservatives were disposed to grant him. The battle cry of the conservatives was therefore "order and discipline." Of the evangelicals it was "the right of conscience." They made a distinction between essential and circumstantial rules. The position of the evangelicals was strikingly similar to that of the Americans in their debate with England after the French and Indian War, for they sought to establish constitutional limitations upon the authority of rulers.

The main questions of polity concern the terms of admission to church-membership and the ministry. In this connection we must consider the charge of censoriousness preferred by the conservatives against the evangelicals. The national churches of England, Scotland, and Holland received candidates into full church-membership if they possessed a competent degree of religious knowledge and lived a moral life. It was hoped that such were converted. The evangelicals assumed that a large percentage of the church-members were unconverted, addressed them as such, and exhorted them to seek clear evidence of conversion. They were also convinced that a majority of the ministers were unconverted, and proclaimed this conviction from the housetops. This attitude to the majority of church-members and ministers was resented by opposers of the revival as uncharitable. Reformers are always charged with censoriousness. Several of the leading evangelists in the beginning, it must be confessed, did show toward their opposers an asperity more exasperating than convincing. As the revival advanced the early narrowness in the definition of conversion was corrected in many, and asperity toward opposers of the revival was quite overcome in such men as Whitefield and Tennent. On the other hand, from the beginning to the end the scurrility and baseness of most publications against the revival were in sharp contrast with the sobriety of most published defenses of the movement.

The opponents of the revival exaggerated beyond measure the bodily agitations which sometimes resulted from the strong emotional appeal of the evangelists. Sudden fears and joys had their natural effect upon persons who were unrestrained by public sentiment from unmeasured expression of their emotion. There was always the danger of the propagation of these phenomena by suggestion. Promoters of the revival sometimes yielded to the temptation of utilizing these commotions to increase the religious excitement.[1] It was a dangerous expedient, but where public sentiment was not arrayed against it more good than evil was the result. Yet sometimes ignorant persons imagined themselves converted because of these physical disturbances, although there was no revulsion against their former manner of life and no passionate surrender to higher aims. In Germany Francke did not at first repress such extravagance but afterward attempted to do so. It was only on very rare occasions that there was any excessive emotionalism in the meetings of Whitefield. Terror had a larger place in Tennent's preaching than in Whitefield's, but he endeavored to curb emotional demonstration. Edwards gave these phenomena qualified approval, but Dickinson set his face against them, and so did the Boston pastors. Warned by the excesses of a few under the frenzied leadership of Davenport, all these promoters of the revival became outspoken against emotional extremes. Very soon Davenport returned to a perfectly sane course and was afterward an effective evangelist in the Presbyterian revival in Virginia. The Separate Baptists of the South inherited from the Separates of Connecticut an enthusiasm which was remarkably effective in the propagation of a religious and moral reformation. The excrescences of this enthusiasm were gradually eliminated in subsequent revivals of the Baptists in those parts, but its fire and force happily long remained.[2]

If there was little ground for the criticism of physical phenomena, still less was there for the criticism of itinerant preaching. Itineracy in the view of the conservatives was unwarranted by Scripture and was destructive of order.[3] This term was applied to the evangelistic journeys of Whitefield and others like him who left their parishes, or were without parishes, and preached in the charges of other ministers as promoters of the revival. The conservatives declared that it was the duty of Whitefield to remain at Savannah, and of Tennent at New Brunswick.[4] Itineracy of this sort was then a novelty and one of the most effective engines of the movement. A large number of gifted men were thus employed in the height of the revival, going from church to church upon

[1] This may have been true of the early preaching of Davenport and Rowland, before they were convinced of their mistaken methods, yet they were probably unconscious of endeavoring directly to produce bodily effects.

[2] Semple, *A History of the . . . . Baptists in Virginia*, p. 59.

[3] Boston *Evening Post*, November 19, 1744.

[4] The first bad thing attending the Work, according to Chauncy, was itinerant preaching. *Seasonable Thoughts*, pp. 36–76.

the invitation of the pastors. Itineracy of another sort was also successfully employed by the New Side Presbyterians. Having few ministers and many vacancies, the ministers and probationers were sent on long journeys, bringing encouragement to many lonely settlements. Later the Methodists reduced this kind of itineracy to a system.

Lay preaching was another measure for the promotion of the revival which was regarded by the conservatives as supremely disorderly. Indeed the Presbyterian and Congregational promoters of the revival agreed with the conservatives in this particular.[1] *Collegia pietatis*, religious societies, bands, and classes were organized among the people. Through these agencies the Great Awakening became a people's movement. Many laymen became effective leaders and forceful speakers. In some of the denominations, as the Separates, Baptists, Moravians, and Methodists, the transition was easy from lay exhorters and lay preachers to ordained ministers. The Methodists and Baptists, by encouraging lay preaching and the advancement of men whose gifts were developed in the school of life, became great popular denominations, while the Presbyterians and Congregationalists, by insisting upon an artificial and unbending requirement, lost the advantage which was given them as the early promoters of the Great Awakening.

Paradoxical as it may seem, the Great Awakening gave a tremendous impulse to education, both ministerial and secular. The Presbyterian, Reformed, and Congregational churches required a thorough educational preparation of candidates for the ministry. There were no public academies in the Middle Colonies. Therefore evangelical ministers bestirred themselves to provide educational facilities for the multitude of gifted young men that the revival thrust forward, to prepare them to preach the gospel. Thus were born not only many private schools, modeled upon the Log College, but chartered schools like the College of New Jersey at Princeton and Queen's College at New Brunswick. A great number of colleges and other educational institutions, westward, northward, and southward, were founded by men whose educational ancestry may be traced back to the Log College. Other schools, from Dartmouth in New Hampshire to Bethesda in Georgia, were fruits of the Great Awakening. Religious bodies like the Separates, Baptists, Moravians, and Methodists, which did not make a diploma an invariable

---

[1] Gilbert Tennent wrote a letter to a minister in Connecticut strongly condemning public and authoritative exhortation and instruction by laymen. He restricts this to men "called of God as Aaron," that is, ordained ministers. He thinks that the itinerations of laymen would lead to dreadful consequences to the churches. Boston *News-Letter*, April 15, 1742.

requirement for ordination, nevertheless coveted the best education possible for their ministers. The energy generated by the revival led to the founding of such schools as Hopewell Academy, Brown University, Nazareth Hall, and Cokesbury College. The evangelicals of every denomination ranked piety higher than intellectual training as a qualification for the ministry. The conservatives therefore everywhere railed against them as the apostles of ignorance. Some promoters of the revival, it is true, in their loyalty to piety decried education. This spirit has survived to the present time in ever-narrowing circles.[1]

So much for the measures employed; doctrine has had little emphasis in this study, but a history of the Great Awakening must make some reference to Luther's doctrine and the relation of this doctrine to moral reform. The evangelicals restored the old Reformation doctrine of justification by faith. The conservatives therefore called them Antinomians.[2] Franklin thought that Andrews, his conservative Presbyterian pastor, neglected moral questions,[3] and Andrews complained of the evangelicals, alleging the same neglect.[4] According to Gilbert Tennent the Moravians were Antinomians.[5] This term was also cast upon the Separates of Connecticut. It was a charge lightly made against all lovers of Luther's doctrine. Only an insignificant number failed to see the necessary connection between Christian experience and right moral conduct.[6] The evangelicals held their followers to a rigorous moral code that greatly promoted the sobriety, industry, and moral progress of the people. But the value of play, even for children, and the need of wholesome diversion were not properly recognized by those stern seekers after the favor of God.[7]

---

[1] The Separates of Connecticut, after the suppression of the Shepherd's Tent at London, decried human learning as related to religious truth. They professed to rely solely on the enlightenment of the Holy Ghost. Blake, *The Separates of New England*, pp. 204–8. The Separate Baptists inherited this view, but the influence of the regular Baptists was strong for education. Ramsay said in 1808 of the South Carolina Baptists, "Among the different sects of christians in South Carolina, none have made earlier or greater exertions for promoting religious knowledge than the baptists" (Ramsay, *South Carolina*, II, 365).

[2] Boston *Evening Post*, January 4, 1742.

[3] Franklin, *Autobiography*, pp. 97–99.

[4] Webster, *A History of the Presbyterian Church*, p. 178.

[5] Gilbert Tennent, *Some Account*, p. 43.   [6] John Cross, for example.

[7] The hours of labor and study of the orphans at Bethesda were regulated. The only recreation apparently was a walk once a day with master or mistress "to bless and admire their great Benefactor" (Creator). *New England Weekly Journal*, September 23, 1740.

While the Great Awakening revived a Puritan rigor, helpful in general but harmful in particulars, a new outlet for the chastened pursuit of happiness was found in the new psalmody.   It was the evangelical revival that gave to the world the songs and melodies of the Moravians, as sensuous and elusive as the Song of Solomon, the "Gospel Sonnets" of the Erskines, the immortal hymns of the Wesleys, and the psalms that made Watts the English David.   The conservatives stormed against the new outburst of song as a profanation.   They even resisted the introduction of improved translations of the Psalms, preferring to wail out the limping lines made sacred by use.[1]

Near to the heart of song is action—friendly, helpful action. Nineteenth-century missions, the glory of the church, had their roots in the new missionary impulse which, like so many other movements, resulted from the Great Awakening.   Christian Rauch and George Post, David Brainerd and John, his brother, Jonathan Edwards, Eleazar Wheelock, and Sampson Occum are but a few names in the list of missionary heroes whom the revival sent to their work.   Missions to the Indians were not born in the Great Awakening, but they were born again and were prosecuted with a whole-heartedness which they had not known since the days of Eliot and the Mayhews.

Humanitarian enterprises of many kinds, besides missionary endeavor, owe their inception to the new social consciousness that came with the Great Awakening.   Sympathies were profoundly stirred. The people were awakened to a new interest in the orphan, the negro, the Indian, and the unfortunate whether at their doors or in the most distant provinces.   The first word against slavery was spoken by men straight from the home of Pietism in Germany.[2]   The antislavery movement in New England was originated by Hopkins, one of the great evangelical leaders.[3]   In the South the New Side Presbyterians and the Baptists at an early day opposed slavery.[4]   The Methodist discipline took strong ground against the system.   Much has been said of Whitefield's owning slaves as an endowment for the orphan house, but not

---

[1] Miller, *Memoirs of the Rev. John Rodgers, D.D.*, pp. 149–53.

[2] Fisher, *The Making of Pennsylvania*, p. 73.

[3] Allen, *Jonathan Edwards*, p. 250.

[4] In 1784 the Christian Conference of Methodists required gradual emancipation by slaveholding members.   In 1787 the synod of New York and Philadelphia adopted a declaration for prudent measures leading to the final abolition of slavery in America. In 1789 the Baptist General Committee of the state of Virginia adopted a strong resolution against slavery.   Tigert, *Constitutional History*, p. 216; Gillett, *History of the Presbyterian Church*, I, 201, 202; Semple, *op. cit.*, p. 105.

enough of his clarion call, heard the whole length of the colonies, demanding for the slave humane treatment and Christian training. The mission to the African in America grew out of the Great Awakening and measurably prepared the negro for the enjoyment of liberty.

The return to the emotional experience of Paul, the doctrine of Luther, and the rigor of John Cotton, with the attendant burst of song and the practical demonstration of the inherent kindliness of the movement, gradually won over nearly every important branch of the Protestant church in America, with one significant exception. The Anglican church in the colonies spurned the aid of Whitefield and impotently pronounced suspension upon him. Wesley's preachers were equally disowned. This church became the last refuge of the conservatives. The Great Awakening built up popular denominations, each with a numerous following of earnest, enthusiastic members. These denominations commanded the respect of the whole American people, even of the irreligious. But the ancient national church of the English people fell into contempt. The Presbyterians and the Congregationalists united in an annual convention to combat what were regarded as the encroachments of the Anglican church, and particularly to prevent the appointment of an American bishop.[1] This was one of the earliest examples of an intercolonial combination to bring pressure to bear upon the English ministry. The Great Awakening was a democratic religious movement, but the Anglican church became more and more a small aristocratic body, centering in an official class. The clergy therefore sought the advancement of their interests by intrigue with the authorities in England. They were suspected by the people of being the emissaries of a foreign government. They shared its fortunes. Thus the revival united with other influences to subvert the Church of England in the colonies.

There is an intimate connection between the American Revolution and the intercolonial religious ferment which preceded it. The policy of the conservatives was divisive and isolating, but the evangelicals almost always advocated union and friendly co-operation.[2] The revival

---

[1] Miller, *op. cit.*, pp. 186–92; *Records of the Presbyterian Church*, p. 373.

[2] When Gilbert Tennent was in London raising money for Princeton College, and Provost Smith was there in the interest of the Philadelphia academy, the former expressed the hope that the college would unite the Presbyterians and German Reformed, but Smith, an Anglican, replied that the union was undesirable. Tennent said, "Union in a good thing is always desirable." Webster, *op. cit.*, p. 394. Though the Great Awakening brought schism to most denominations, the cause was not the divisive measures of the evangelicals but the hostility of the conservatives, who expelled the evangelicals, or forced their withdrawal, or themselves withdrew. Reunion, when effected, was due to the efforts of the evangelicals.

spirit was always the foe of denominational and racial prejudices. The Great Awakening widened the horizon of the people, for it was the first intellectual movement in which all the colonies participated. Denominations that were aggressively evangelistic ignored provincial boundaries and built up constituencies which were intercolonial in character. The revival led to a very considerable movement of population.[1] This helped create a common American spirit. The Anglican church was one of the ties uniting the colonies with the mother country. The combination against that church and the winning of a large part of its nominal membership weakened that tie. The community of feeling which the revival cultivated in the several Calvinistic bodies, the actual combination of some of them against the English church, and the fear of invasion by the English government of their religious liberties were evidences of a spiritual union of the colonies which was prophetic of a national union. In just the same way a century later the disruption of the great popular denominations upon a sectional question was prophetic of the Civil War. The Great Awakening prepared the way for the Revolutionary War. The denominations, like the Presbyterian and the Baptist, which were built up by the revival took almost unanimously the patriot side. It was their meeting-houses that were burned as nests of rebellion and their pastors that were hunted as instigators of treason.[2]

The separation of church and state was an application of the principles of the Great Awakening and the Revolution. The democratic principles of both were contrary to the special privileges of established churches. The growth of great bodies which did not possess these privileges, like the Presbyterian and Baptist denominations, raised up powerful organizations which did not rest until every vestige of an establishment was erased from the statute books. This was the course in Virginia[3] and other southern provinces. It was so in New York, where a law, passed by dissenters in their own interest, had been interpreted as the establishment of the Church of England in parts of the province. The same fate befell the churches of the standing order in Massachusetts and Connecticut.

While the quickening of the religious life was so far arrested by the social and political disturbances accompanying the Revolution that the

[1] Particularly that of Separates and Baptists from Connecticut and other eastern states to Vermont and New York. In its results the little colony of Separate Baptists which moved to Virginia and North Carolina was of prime importance.

[2] Breed, *Presbyterians and the Revolution;* Gillett, *op. cit.,* I, 173–98.

[3] Eckenrode, *Separation of Church and State in Virginia,* pp. 37, 129, 147.

Great Awakening may be said then to have come to an end, yet as a force in America the evangelical revival has never had an end. It burst into flame again in the revivals at the close of the eighteenth century and was dominant in American religious life for a hundred years after the Revolutionary War.[1]

A final word as to the Middle Colonies, with which this study has been primarily concerned. The Great Awakening found them in a state of confusion, in a tangle of warring sects and hostile nationalities. Its partisans slowly gained the control of nearly all these denominations and brought them into united effort for common religious and political ends. Its leaders were in hearty accord with Edwards, Bellamy, and their sympathizers in the Connecticut Valley and with the evangelical pastors of Boston. They also conducted religious campaigns in the South. The more democratic promoters of revivalism, likewise from the Middle Colonies, reached out to the South to make converts and to New England to effect union with their coreligionists. Thus the Middle Colonies were the center of a movement which bound together the whole line of colonies, at first religiously and socially, and then politically.[2] All the features of this intercolonial and world-wide movement enumerated in this chapter are therefore illustrated by the history of the Great Awakening in the Middle Colonies.

[1] Hoskins, "German Influence on Religious Life and Thought in America in the Colonial Period," *Princeton Theological Review*, V (1907).

[2] Of course the Great Awakening was not the only force in the process of nation-making, but its contribution was highly significant, especially in determining what is typically American in the sphere of religion.

BIBLIOGRAPHY

Alexander, A. *Biographical Sketches of the Founder and Principal Alumni of the Log College.* Philadelphia, 1851.

Allen, A. V. G. *Jonathan Edwards.* Boston, 1890.

Asbury, F. *Journal.* 3 vols. New York.

Beadle, E. R. *The Old and the New: 1743-1876.* Philadelphia, 1876.

Beatty, C. *Double Honour.* Sermon at ordination of W. Ramsey. Philadelphia, 1757.

Bellamy, Joseph. *True Religion Delineated; or Experimental Religion.* Boston, 1750.

Benedict, D. *A General History of the Baptist Denomination.* 2 vols. Boston 1813.

Billingsley, A. S. *The Life of the Great Preacher Reverend George Whitefield.* Philadelphia, 1878.

Blair, John. *The New Creation.* Philadelphia, 1767.

Blair, Samuel. *The Great Glory of God.* Boston, 1739.

———. *A Persuasion to Repentance.* Philadelphia, 1743(?).

———. *A Sermon . . . . Funeral of the Reverend Mr. William Robinson.* Philadelphia, 1746.

———. *Works.* Philadelphia, 1754.

Blake, S. L. *The Separates of New England.* Boston, 1902.

Bolles, A. S. *Pennsylvania Province and State.* 2 vols. Philadelphia, 1899.

Bradford, A. *Memoir of the Life and Writings of Rev. Jonathan Mayhew, D.D.* Boston, 1838.

Brainerd, David. Memoirs in Vol. X of *The Works of President Edwards.* New York, 1829.

Brainerd, T. *The Life of John Brainerd.* Philadelphia, 1865.

Breed, W. P. *Presbyterians and the Revolution.* Philadelphia, 1876.

Briggs, C. A. *American Presbyterianism.* New York, 1885.

Brown, A. H. *An Outline History of the Presbyterian Churches in West or South Jersey from 1700 to 1865.* Philadelphia, 1869.

Brumbaugh, M. G. *A History of the German Baptist Brethren.* Elgin, 1899.

Buell, Samuel. *A Copy of a Letter . . . . to the Rev. Mr. Barber of Groton in Conn.* 1764.

———. *A Faithful Narrative of the Remarkable Revival of Religion in the Congregation of Easthampton on Long Island.* 1808.

Burr, A. *A Sermon . . . . Ordination of the Reverend Mr. David Bostwick* New York, 1745.

Centennial Memorial of the Presbytery of Carlisle, The. 2 vols. Harrisburg, 1889.

Chanler, Isaac. *The Doctrine of Glorious Grace.* Boston, 1744.

Chapell, F. L. *The Great Awakening of 1740.* Philadelphia, 1903.

Chauncy, C. *Seasonable Thoughts.* Boston, 1743.

Cleveland, C. C. *The Great Revival in the West, 1797–1805.* Chicago, 1916.

Colton, C. *History and Character of American Revivals.* London, 1832.

Confessions of Faith . . . . Church of Scotland, The. Glasgow, 1771.

Corwin, E. T. *Historical Discourse . . . . Millstone.* New York, 1866.

——. *A Manual of the Reformed Church in America.* New York, 1879.

Davenport, F. M. *Primitive Traits in Religious Revivals.* New York, 1905.

Davenport, James. *The Faithful Minister Encouraged.* Philadelphia, 1756.

Davies, Samuel. *The Duties, Difficulties and Rewards of the faithful Minister.* Glasgow, 1754.

——. *A Sermon on Man's Primitive State.* Philadelphia, 1748.

——. *Little Children invited to Jesus Christ.* Boston, 1798.

——. *The State of Religion in Virginia.* Boston, 1751.

——. *Sermons*, with funeral sermon by Samuel Finley. Philadelphia, 1864.

Demerest, D. D. *The Huguenots on the Hackensack.* New Brunswick, 1886.

——. *The Reformed Dutch Church in America.* New York, 1889.

Dickinson, Jonathan. *Familiar Letters.* Boston, 1745.

——. (attributed). *Remarks upon a Discourse intituled An Overture.* New York, 1729.

——. *A Sermon Preached at the Opening of the Synod.* Boston, 1722(?).

——. *A Vindication of God's sovereign free Grace.* Boston, 1746.

Dubbs, J. H. *The Reformed Church, German.* New York, 1895.

Dwight, S. E. *Memoirs of Jonathan Edwards.* Vol. I of *The Works of President Edwards.* New York, 1829.

Ecclesiastical Records of the State of New York, published under the supervision of H. Hastings, Albany, 1902.

Eckenrode, H. J. *Separation of Church and State in Virginia.* Richmond, 1910.

Edwards, Jonathan (S. E. Dwight, editor). *The Works of President Edwards.* New York, 1829.

Edwards, Morgan. *Material toward a History of the American Baptists.* Philadelphia, 1770.

Evans, David. *The Minister of Christ.* Philadelphia, 1732.

Field, R. S. "Review of the Trial of the Rev. William Tennent for Perjury in 1742," *Proceedings of the New Jersey Historical Society.* Vol. VI. Newark, 1853.

Finley, James. *An Essay on the Gospel Ministry.* Wilmington, 1763.

Finley, Samuel. *Christ triumphing and Satan raging.* Philadelphia, 1741.
————. *The Madness of Mankind.* Philadelphia, 1754(?).
————. *The Successful Minister.* Sermon delivered at the funeral of Gilbert Tennent. Philadelphia, 1764.

Fisher, S. G. *The Making of Pennsylvania.* Philadelphia, 1896.

Foote, E. J. *A Sketch of the Life of Rev. Abel Morgan.* In the minutes of the Trenton Baptist Association. Trenton, 1883.

Fox, George. *A Journal.* Philadelphia.

Franklin, B. *Autobiography.* New York: Burt Co.

Frelinghuysen, T. J. *Sermons.* New York, 1856.

Futhey, J. S. *Historical Discourse . . . . Upper Octorara Presbyterian Church.* Philadelphia, 1870.

Garden, A. *Six Letters to the Reverend G. Whitefield.* New York, 1740.

Gib, Adam. *A Warning against . . . . George Whitefield.* Edinburgh, 1742.

Gillespie, G. *A Letter to the . . . . Presbytery of New York.* Philadelphia, 1742.

Gillett, E. H. *History of the Presbyterian Church.* Philadelphia, 1864.

Gillies, J. *Historical Collections.* Kelso, 1845.
————. *Memoirs of Rev. George Whitefield.* Middletown, 1836.

Gledstone, J. P. *George Whitefield.* Second edition. New York.

Gordon, T. F. *The History of Pennsylvania.* Philadelphia, 1829.

Green, A. *The Life and Death of the Righteous.* Sermon delivered at the funeral of Rev. W. M. Tennent, D.D. Philadelphia, 1811.

Green, H. W. (attributed). "The Trial of the Rev. William Tennent," *Princeton Review.* Philadelphia, July, 1868.

Gunn, A. *Memoirs of the Rev. John H. Livingston, D.D.* New York, 1829.

Hale, G. *A History of the Old Presbyterian Congregations of the People of Maidenhead and Hopewell.* Philadelphia, 1876.

Hall, J. *History of the Presbyterian Church in Trenton.* New York, 1859.

Hamilton, J. T. *The Moravian Church in the United States.* 1894.

Hamilton, T. *History of the Irish Presbyterian Church.* Edinburgh, 1887.

Hanna, C. A. *The Scotch-Irish.* New York, 1902.

Hodge, C. *The Constitutional History of the Presbyterian Church.* In two parts. Philadelphia, 1851.

Hoskins, J. P. "German Influence on Religious Life and Thought in America during the Colonial Period," *Princeton Theological Review.* Vol. V. Princeton, 1907.

Ingram, G. H. "The Erection of the Presbytery of New Brunswick," *Journal of the Presbyterian Historical Society.* Philadelphia, June, 1912.

Jacobs, H. E. *Lutherans.* New York, 1893.

Kahm, Peter. *Travels into North America.* Warrington, 1790.

Kaufmann, M. "Latitudinarianism and Pietism" in Vol. V, *The Age of Louis XIV,* "Cambridge Modern History." New York, 1912.

Keen, W. W. *The First Baptist Church of Philadelphia.* Philadelphia, 1899.

Kuhns, O. *The German and Swiss Settlements of Colonial Pennsylvania.* New York, 1901.

Late Religious Commotions in New England considered, The. Boston, 1743.

Letter from a Gentleman in Boston to Mr. George Wishart, A. Edinburgh, 1742.

Livingston, W. *The Independent Reflector.* New York, 1753.

MS Minutes of the New Brunswick Presbytery (from 1738).

MS Records of the Second Presbyterian Church of Philadelphia (from 1743).

McConnell, S. D. *History of the American Episcopal Church.* New York, 1890.

Macpherson, J. *A History of the Church in Scotland.* Paisley, 1901.

Messler, A. *Eight Memorial Sermons.* With historical notes. New York, 1873.

————. *The Hollander in New Jersey.*

Miller, S. *Memoirs of Rev. John Rodgers, D.D.* New York, 1829.

Mirbt, C. "Pietism" in Vol. IX of *New Schaff-Herzog Religious Encyclopedia.* New York, 1909.

Morgan, J. *The General Causes of all hurtful Mistakes.* Philadelphia, 1741.

Murphy, T. *The Presbytery of the Log College.* Philadelphia, 1889.

Nevin, A. *History of the Presbytery of Philadelphia.* Philadelphia, 1888.

Newspapers (for the period of the Great Awakening, especially for the years 1736–46):

> The Boston *News-Letter.*
>
> The Boston *Gazette.*
>
> The *New England Weekly Journal,* Boston.
>
> The Boston *Weekly Post-Boy.*
>
> The Boston *Evening Post.*
>
> The New York *Gazette.*
>
> The New York *Weekly Journal.*
>
> The New York *Post-Boy.*
>
> The *American Weekly Mercury,* Philadelphia.
>
> The *Pennsylvania Gazette,* Philadelphia.
>
> The *Weekly Advertiser or Pennsylvania Journal,* Philadelphia.
>
> The *Maryland Gazette,* Annapolis.
>
> The *Virginia Gazette,* Williamsburg.
>
> The *South Carolina Gazette,* Charleston.

Pemberton, E. *Heaven . . . . Death of the Rev. George Whitefield.* Boston, 1771.

Pennypacker, S. W. *Origin of the University of Pennsylvania in 1740.* Philadelphia, 1899.

Prime, E. *The Pastor at Large.* New York, 1758.

Prince, Thomas, Jr. (editor). *The Christian History* for the years 1743 and 1744. Boston.

Querists, The. New York, 1740.

Ramsay, D. *The History of South Carolina*, 2 vols. Charleston, 1809.

Ravenel, H. H. *Eliza Pinckney.* New York, 1896.

Records of the Presbyterian Church. Philadelphia, 1841.

Reed and Matheson. *A Narrative of a Visit.* 2 vols. New York, 1835.

Ritter, A. *History of the Moravian Church in Philadelphia.* Philadelphia, 1857.

Robe, J. *The Christian Monthly History.* Edinburgh, 1743.

Rowland, John. *A Narrative of the Revival . . . . in . . . . Hopewell, Amwell and Maidenhead . . . . and New-Providence.* Philadelphia, 1745.

Sachse, J. F. *The German Pietists of Provincial Pennsylvania.* Philadelphia, 1895.

———. *The German Sectarians of Pennsylvania.* Philadelphia, 1899.

Semple, R. B. (G. W. Beale, editor). *A History of the . . . . Baptists in Virginia.* Richmond, 1894.

Seward, William. *Journal of a Voyage.* London, 1740.

Smith, G. G. *Life and Letters of James Osgood Andrew.* 1883.

Smith, Robert, and Finley, Samuel. *The Detection Detected.* Lancaster, 1757.

Spangenberg, A. G. *The Life of Count Zinzendorf.* London, 1838.

Sprout, J. *A Discourse* on the death of Whitefield. Philadelphia, 1771.

Stearns, J. F. *Historical Discourses Relating to the First Presbyterian Church in Newark.* Newark, 1853.

Steele, R. H. *Historical Discourse.* New Brunswick, 1867.

Stevens, G. *The Psychology of the Christian Soul.* New York, 1911.

Stiles, E. *The Literary Diary.* New York, 1901.

Symmes, F. R. *History of the Old Tennent Church.* Cranbury, 1904.

Talmage, G. *A Sermon.* With historical and statistical statements. New York, 1862.

Tennent, Gilbert, *All Things come alike to all.* Philadelphia, 1745.

———. *The Blessedness of Peace-Makers represented; and the Danger of Persecution considered.* Two sermons. Philadelphia, 1765.

———. *Brotherly Love Recommended.* Philadelphia, 1748.

———. *The Danger of an Unconverted Ministry.* Boston, 1742.

———. MS Defense of Notes, 1762.

———. *Discourses on Several Important Subjects.* Philadelphia, 1745.

———. *The Divine Government.* Philadelphia, 1752.

———. *The Examiner Examined.* Philadelphia, 1743.

———. *An Expostulatory Address.* London, 1741.

———. *A Funeral Sermon . . . . Rev. John Rowland.* Philadelphia, 1745.

———. *The Good Man's Character.* Delivered at the funeral of Captain Grant. Philadelphia, 1756(?).

———. *Irenicum Ecclesiasticum.* Philadelphia, 1749.

Tennent, Gilbert. *The Late Association.* Argument against the Quakers. Philadelphia, 1748.

―――. *The Late Association . . . . farther encouraged.* Philadelphia, 1748.

―――. *The Late Association for Defence.* Philadelphia, 1747.

―――. *The Necessity of holding fast the Faith.* Argument against the Moravians. Boston, 1743.

―――. MS Remonstrance. 1762.

―――. *A Sermon . . . . Day appointed by . . . . President and Council . . . . as Day of Fasting and Prayer.* Philadelphia, 1748.

―――. *A Sermon . . . . On Occasion of . . . . Victory . . . . over . . . . Fleets of France and Spain.* Philadelphia, 1744.

―――. *Sermon Preached . . . . to Captain Vanderspiegel's Independent Company of Volunteers.* Philadelphia, 1756.

―――. *Some Account of the Principles of the Moravians.* London, 1743.

―――. *Two Sermons . . . . at Burlington.* Dedicated to Governor Belcher. Philadelphia, 1749.

―――. *The Unsearchable Riches of Christ.* Boston, 1739.

Tennent, John. *The Nature of Regeneration opened.* London, 1741.

Tennent, William (Sr.). MS Sacramental Sermon. 1717.

Tennent, William (Jr.). *An Exhortation to Walk in Christ.* Boston, 1739.

Tennent, William (III). *An Address . . . . Invasion of Liberties.* Philadelphia, 1774.

Thomas, I. *History of Printing in America.* Albany, 1874.

Thompson, D. D. *John Wesley as a Social Reformer.* New York, 1898.

Thompson, R. E. *Presbyterians.* New York, 1895.

Tigert, J. J. *Constitutional History of American Episcopal Methodism.* Nashville, 1894.

Tracy, Joseph. *The Great Awakening: A History of the Revival of Religion in the Time of Edwards and Whitefield.* Boston, 1842.

Tyerman, L. *The Life and Times of Rev. John Wesley.* 3 vols. New York, 1872.

―――. *The Life of the Rev. George Whitefield.* 2 vols. New York, 1877.

Vedder, H. C. *A History of the Baptists in the Middle States.* Philadelphia, 1898.

Watson, J. F. *Annals of Philadelphia.* Philadelphia, 1891.

Webster, R. *A History of the Presbyterian Church.* Philadelphia, 1857.

Wheelock, Eleazar. *A plain and faithful Narrative.* Boston, 1763.

―――. *A Continuation.* Boston, 1765.

Whitefield, George. *Brief Account of the First Part of his Life.* Philadelphia, 1740.

―――. *A Further Account.* London, 1747.

―――. *A Journal* (No. 1). London, 1743

―――. *A Continuation* (No. 2). London, 1739.

―――. *A Continuation* (No. 3). London, 1739.

Whitefield, George.　*A Continuation* (No. 4).　London, 1739.

———.　*A Continuation* (No. 5).　London, 1740.

———.　*A Continuation* (No. 6).　London, 1741.

———.　*A Continuation* (No. 7).　London, 1744.

———.　MS Journal for 1744.

———.　*A Letter .. . . . In Answer to . . . . Querists.*　New York, 1740.

———.　*Some Remarks on a Pamphlet.*　Philadelphia, 1749.

———.　*A Letter to his Excellency Governor Wright.*　London, 1768.

NOTE.—The dates of publications given are of the editions used in the preparation of this study.　Many books and manuscripts have been consulted in addition to those given in the preceding list.